Kali S. Banerjee

On the Factorial Approach Providing the True Index of Cost of Living

Angewandte Statistik und Ökonometrie
Applied Statistics and Econometrics
Statistique Appliquée et Econométrie

Herausgegeben von / Edited by / publié par

Robert Feron, Gerhard Tintner,
Pierre Désiré Thionet, Heinrich Strecker

Heft 5

Vandenhoeck & Ruprecht in Göttingen

On the Factorial Approach Providing the True Index of Cost of Living

by

Kali S. Banerjee

2nd enlarged edition

Vandenhoeck & Ruprecht in Göttingen

To Shri Gopal Gobinda
Goswami Acharyya

CIP-Kurztitelaufnahme der Deutschen Bibliothek

Banerjee, Kali S.:
On the factorial approach providing the true index of cost of living / by Kali S. Banerjee. – 2., enlarged ed. – Göttingen : Vandenhoeck & Ruprecht, 1980.
(Angewandte Statistik und Ökonometrie ; H. 5)

ISBN 3-525-11248-3

2nd enlarged edition 1980
 Druck: Hubert & Co., Göttingen.

Contents

CHAPTER ONE

INTRODUCTION

1.1 Status of the Classical Theory of Economic Price Indices: It is well known that the True Index of Cost of Living (or the Economic Price Index), as envisaged in the economic theory of Price Indices,[1] is a highly abstract concept, not capable of exact measurement. A unique Price Index Formula, as conceived of in the set-up of maximization of ordinal utility in the theory of consumer choice, is unknown.

An account of the complexities of the problem is found in Frisch [13] and Staehle[23]. For a general treatment of this subject field, we may refer to Samuelson [21], Wold and Jureen [28], and Malmquist [18], and for some specific issues, to Fisher and Shell [11]. To provide a simple definition, - a definition that has taken a concrete shape over the years, - we may say that the true index of cost of living is the ratio of (minimum) costs of a given level of living (standard of living, or the general status of "want satisfaction") in two price situations. Questions arise as to whether we should choose the indifference map of the base period (reference period) or of the current period (the period compared) for the given level of living, because the index will depend upon the choice of the indifference map. The two indices will differ, and thus there will be two different indices for a comparison between two price situations.

The pioneers in this field, like Konüs [17], Frisch [13], Staehle [23], Haberler [14], among others, have provided working conditions to approximate such an index, but those approximating conditions have not apparently led, so far, to a practicable solution of the problem.

Contemporary economists, like Allen [2], Hicks [15], Samuelson and Swamy [20], Afriat [1], Pollak [19],

---

[1]In this review, the words "Indices" and "Indexes" have been synonymously used to denote the plural.

Fisher and Shell [11], Theil [25], Kloek and DeWit [16], Stuvel [24], Geary [13A], Gorman [13B], Khamis [15B] and Klein and Rubin [15C], among others, continue to provide guide lines for the "true index" of cost of living, but the actual construction remains as conceptual as ever.

Wald [26] is perhaps the first among those, who have worked in this area, to provide such a Price Index Formula in an exact form. However, the formula is worked out under the simplifying assumption of permissibility to approximate the utility function by a second degree polynomial. The formula is eventually expressed in terms of the coefficients of Engel Curves (linear).

It is generally recognized that it is not possible to provide such a Price Index Formula in concrete terms, unless the utility function is specified. The True Index of Cost of Living refers to a constant level of utility, and is, thus, a function of the particular level of the utility to which the Index relates. Consistent with this requirement of "constant utility," no unique Price Index Formula exists between the two price situations, sought to be compared, unless the utility function is <u>homothetic</u> to the origin, in which case, however, the True Index of Cost of Living goes independent of the level of utility (see Samuelson and Swamy [20]).

But, then again, the assumption of <u>homothetic preference</u> imposes a serious restriction on the form of the utility function. Such a restriction, therefore, detracts from the general character of the Index Number Formula. It has thus become amply evident over the years that the classical theory of price indices cannot provide a unique formula of a general nature. It is against this perspective that the "factorial approach" to the True Index of Cost of Living is to be viewed.

1.2 <u>The Factorial Approach</u>: The factorial approach was detailed in a couple of papers [3,4] a few years ago. The formula for the True Index of Cost of Living, as provided by this approach, is simple and easy to apply.

The "factorial approach" is characterized by the same Gauss-Markoff least squares principles which pave the foundation of "factorial experiments." The estimation procedure is anologous to the methodology usually adopted in the analysis of a 2^2-factorial experiment. The Price and the Quantity are the two factors with "0" and "1" as their levels, where "0" refers to the base period, and "1" to the period compared.

The structure, on which the least squares principles are applied, utilizes the Divisia index permitting Σpq to be expressed as $\overset{*}{P}\overset{*}{Q}$, where "$\overset{*}{P}$" refers to the general level of prices, and "$\overset{*}{Q}$" to the physical volume of goods. Divisia indexes thus provide the connecting link between the "factorial approach," on one hand, and the general theory of economic price indices on the other. (See Hulten [15A])

A point q_1 in the period 1 is defined to be equivalent in satisfaction to the point q_0 in the period 0, if the quantity index of q_1 compared to q_0 is unity. This condition of "unity quantity index" comes out as the same as the condition that would show that the "quantity effect" is zero. This condition is then utilized to evaluate the "true index" of cost of living. The "true index," thus obtained, lies between Laspeyres' price index and Paasche's price index [9]. We mention this fact here because there is a strong presumption that if a unique formula for the "true index" of cost of living is to exist, it would lie between these limits. Such a presumption is reflected particularly in the investigations of Konüs [17] and, in a way, also in the work of Staehle [23], to name only two of the leading pioneers.

Then again, the same "factorial approach" formulation gives the basis for evaluating the "true index" of quantity (economic quantity index) as well. The "true index" of quantity lies between Laspeyres' quantity index and Paasche's quantity index.

1.3 What the Factorial Approach Provides: It may be mentioned that, besides paving a basis for formulating the "true index" of cost of living and the "true index" of quantity, the "factorial approach" provides various generalizations including the construction of multi-dimensional indexes.

In the set-up of factorial experiments, it is easy to recognize that the value change can be thought of as the sum of two orthogonal components (independent), one due to price and the other due to quantity. This property is then exploited to split the index of National Income or value change into two independent components of price and quantity as discussed in [3].

In developing multidimensional indexes in [7], we utilized a special subset of the treatment combinations of a 2^n-factorial experiment. The fractional plan coming from this subset has been called the "Index Plan." How such a fractional replicate behaves in the context of fractional replicates in Design of Experiments in general is studied in [8].

More importantly, the factorial approach provides a new interpretation to Stuvel's indexes [24] which were found earlier by Stuvel [24] on an intuitive basis, while working out a method for obtaining unbiased measures of the effect of change in the terms of trade on a country's foreign balance on current account. In view of the close relationship of the factorial approach with Stuvel's formulation, a generalization of the averaging procedure of Stuvel's approach was worked out in [6].

The connection of the factorial approach with Theil's [25] "best linear index numbers" is traced in [5].

In fact, it has been demonstrated in [4] that this methodology can be utilized to provide a "unified statistical approach" to index number problems in general.

1.4 Aim of the Present Review: In the present review, we start with the derivation of Stuvel's new indexes in Chapter Two, with which the "factorial approach" is closely connected, and we spell out in Chapter Three the requisite least squares model and reproduce the formulation of the problem of evaluating the "true index" of cost of living (or the Economic Price Index). In Chapter Four, we discuss the derivation of "multidimensional indexes" the basis of which is provided by the "factorial approach." Chapter Five shows the connection of the factorial indexes with Theil's best linear unbiased index numbers. In view of the importance of Stuvel's new indexes, we present in Chapter Six a generalization of Stuvel's [24] averaging procedure providing additional index number formulae.

A numerical table is provided in Chapter Three showing how we can split the National Income of a country into two orthogonal components, - one due to price and the other due to quantity. This statistical table is a reproduction of a table indicated earlier in [3] except for some of its columns. The additional columns are incorporated in this table to illustrate the calculation of the "true index" of cost of living (economic price index) and economic quantity index. It has become possible to illustrate the calculation of such economic indices from the National Income data, as these data furnish the same kind of expenditure totals which are needed for the calculation of such indices.

The methodology of the "factorial approach" is extended [9C] in Chapter Seven to provide index number formulae for price and quantity over an arbitrary number of periods (or geographical units). The formulae reduce to what are obtained in Chapter Two (or Chapter Three) when the number of periods n=2. Two simple numerical examples are presented in this Chapter illustrating the calculations. The "factorial approach" gives rise to six pairs of equations giving six sets of price and quantity indexes. One of these six pairs of equations is discussed in detail in Chapter Eight, as this pair of equations appears to have a special interest [9A,9D]. Chapter Nine spells out explicitly [9E] the connection of the "factorial indexes" with the "Divisia Integral Indexes," reiterating the fact that the "factorial approach",while being meaningful on its own right, assumes a special significance by virtue of its association with the Divisia Integral Indexes. Finally, in Chapter Ten, we present an algebraic as well as an empirical comparison [9F] between the factorial "true index" and the "true index" of price (economic price index,or the constant-utility "ture index" of price,or the "true index" of cost of living), as given by the Klein-Rubin [15C] or the Geary/Stone [13A,23A] form of the utility function and the "true index" of cost of living, provided by quadratic approximation of the utility function, as given by Wald [26]. The agreement is demonstrated to be remarkable in each case.

CHAPTER TWO

STUVEL'S NEW INDEXES

2.0 Chapter Summary: Stuvel's new indexes are presented in this chapter. The entire derivation, which is linked with the "factorial approach," is reproduced here retaining Stuvel's own language and notations. The indexes satisfy the time reversal and the factor reversal tests.

2.1 Stuvel's Derivation: "Recently, while working out a method for obtaining unbiased measures of the effect of changes in the terms of trade on a country's foreign balance on current account,[2] I stumbled, as it were, on what I believe to be a new index number formula. For volume (q_n) and price (p_n), respectively, this formula reads:

$$(2.1) \qquad q_n = \frac{L-\Lambda}{2} + \sqrt{\left(\frac{L-\Lambda}{2}\right)^2 + \frac{V_n}{V_0}}$$

and

$$(2.2) \qquad p_n = \frac{\Lambda-L}{2} + \sqrt{\left(\frac{\Lambda-L}{2}\right)^2 + \frac{V_n}{V_0}}$$

in which L and Λ denote the Laspeyres or base-weighted indices of volume and price, respectively, and V_n and V_0 the values of the aggregate in the current year n and in the base year o.

On closer examination it appears that this q_n and p_n possess practically all the properties of the quantity and price relatives for single commodities and that also in some respects they are superior to other types of index number. Among other things, they meet the two tests set by Fisher for an "ideal" index number, namely, the time-reversal test and the factor-reversal test. Before

---

[2]See my paper on "A New Approach to the Measurement of Terms-of-Trade Effects" in The Review of Economics and Statistics, August, 1956, and "The Impact of Changes in the Terms of Trade on Western Europe's Balance of Payments" to be published in a later issue of Econometrica.

demonstrating this, however, I propose to explain first the conceptual origin of these new index numbers and to show how their formulae have been arrived at.

For simplicity's sake, I will couch the following argument in terms of intertemporal comparison of commodity flows. The use of these new index numbers, however, is not confined to intertemporal comparisons and to flow analysis only. <u>Mutatis</u> <u>mutandis</u> the argument proves equally applicable to interspatial comparisons and to stock analysis, or indeed to practically any other type of analysis in which index numbers play a part.

The value V of the transactions in any given commodity i during any given period, be it the base year 0 or the current year n, is equal to the product of quantity Q and price P. Consequently the value of the transactions in this commodity in the current year, V_n^i, can be related to the value of the transactions in this commodity in the base year, V_0^i, through multiplication of the latter value with the appropriate volume and price relatives (q_n^i and p_n^i, which are equal to Q_n^i/Q_0^i and P_n^i/P_0^i, respectively). Thus

$$(2.3) \qquad V_n^i = V_0^i q_n^i p_n^i \quad \text{for} \quad \frac{V_n^i}{V_0^i} = \frac{Q_n^i P_n^i}{Q_0^i P_0^i} .$$

However, this type of analysis of value developments V_n^i/V_0^i into a volume and a price component (q_n^i and p_n^i, respectively), which may be called a multiplicative analysis of value developments, is not the only way in which current-year values can be related to base-year values. For certain problems, e.g., the measurement of terms of trade effects, it proves necessary to analyse the difference (not the ratio) between the current-year value and the base-year value ($V_n^i - V_0^i$) into two or more additive components of change. For present purposes it is sufficient to make a distinction between two such additive components, namely A^i which measures how much of the value change is due to a change in volume, and B^i which measures how much is the result of price change.

For this alternative type of analysis, which may be called an additive analysis of value changes, two different formulae suggest themselves, for one has the choice of using either the base-year volume valued at the current-year price, $Q_0^iP_n^i = V_0^ip_n^i$, or the current-year volume valued at the base-year price, $Q_n^iP_0^i=V_n^i/p_n^i=V_0^iq_n^i$, as a means of separating the volume effect from the price effect. The formulae concerned read as follows:

$$(2.4)\quad V_n^i-V_0^i=(V_n^i-V_0^ip_n^i)+(V_0^ip_n^i-V_0^i)=V_0^ip_n^i(q_n^i-1)+V_0^i(p_n^i-1)$$

and

$$(2.5)\quad V_n^i-V_0^i=(V_n^i-V_0^iq_n^i)+(V_0^iq_n^i-V_0^i)=V_0^iq_n^i(p_n^i-1)+V_0^i(q_n^i-1).$$

As I explained in my article in The Review of Economics and Statistics, the measures obtained for each of the two components by means of either of these formulae are biased in a sense, and the most suitable procedure for removing this bias is to average all conceivable measures for each of the components concerned. For the particular case we are dealing with here this means averaging of the measures given in formulae (2.4) and (2.5). Consequently we end up with the following formula[3]:

$$(2.6)\qquad V_n^i-V_0^i = V_0^i\,\frac{p_n^i+1}{2}\,(q_n^i-1)+V_0^i\,\frac{q_n^i+1}{2}\,(p_n^i-1)=A^i+B^i$$

where

$$A^i \equiv V_0^i\,\frac{p_n^i+1}{2}\,(q_n^i-1)$$

---

[3]This formula is consistent with the more general formula presented in my Review of Economics and Statistics article. There I distinguished four instead of two additive components of change (volume level, volume pattern, price level, and price structure), and discussed more fully the nature of the bias and the justification of the averaging procedure as a means of removing it.

is the value change resulting from volume change measured at the average price (i.e., the average of the current-year and base-year price) and

$$B^i \equiv V_0^i \frac{q_n^i+1}{2} (p_n^i-1)$$

the value change due to price change measured with reference to the average volume.

Since formula (2.6) holds for each single commodity (i) we may write for a group of commodities (i=1,...,m)

$$(2.7) \quad \sum_i V_n^i - \sum_i V_0^i = \sum_i V_0^i \frac{p_n^i+1}{2} (q_n^i-1) + \sum_i V_0^i \frac{q_n^i+1}{2} (p_n^i-1) =$$

$$= \sum_i A^i + \sum_i B^i \; .$$

From the point of view of macro-economic analysis it is clearly desirable to obtain the same result directly by means of a formula like (2.6) in which index numbers of volume and price for the aggregate, q_n and p_n, take the place of the volume and price relatives for a single commodity, q_n^i and p_n^i.

After rewriting formula (2.7) as

$$(2.8) \qquad V_n - V_0 = A + B,$$

where

$$V_n \equiv \sum_i V_n^i, \quad V_0 \equiv \sum_i V_0^i, \quad A \equiv \sum_i A^i \text{ and } B \equiv \sum_i B^i,$$

the conditions such index numbers would have to satisfy appear to be that

$$(2.9) \quad V_0 \frac{p_n+1}{2} (q_n-1) = A \quad \text{and} \quad V_0 \frac{q_n+1}{2} (p_n-1) = B.$$

In other words, the index numbers of volume and price to be applied in the additive analysis of the change in value of a group of commodities between the base year and the current year should be such that the resulting volume component and price component are each equal to the sum of the corresponding components in the value changes of the individual commodities in the group between the base year and the current year.

For establishing the formulae of these index numbers, formula (2.9) provides the obvious starting point. By respectively adding and subtracting the expressions for A and B given there we find that

$$V_0(q_n p_n - 1) = A+B \tag{2.10}$$

and

$$V_0(q_n - p_n) = A-B. \tag{2.11}$$

Furthermore, with the help of formula (2.8) we can transform formula (2.10) into

$$q_n p_n = V_n/V_0 \tag{2.12}$$

and by substituting in this formula the expression for p_n which results from formula (2.11) we arrive at

$$q_n^2 + \frac{B-A}{V_0} q_n - \frac{V_n}{V_0} = 0. \tag{2.13}$$

One of the roots of this quadratic equation in q_n is

$$q_n = \frac{A-B}{2V_0} + \sqrt{\left(\frac{A-B}{2V_0}\right)^2 + \frac{V_n}{V_0}} \tag{2.14}$$

to which according to formula (2.11) corresponds the following formula for p_n:

$$p_n = \frac{B-A}{2V_0} + \sqrt{\left(\frac{B-A}{2V_0}\right)^2 + \frac{V_n}{V_0}}\ . \tag{2.15}$$

The other root of (2.13), in which the second term in the expression for q_n would be negative - instead of positive as in (2.14) - has to be rejected, for it would make q_n negative ($V_n/V_0 > 0$ and $\left(\frac{A-B}{2V_0}\right)^2 > 0$, hence

$$|\sqrt{(\frac{A-B}{2V_0})^2 + \frac{V_n}{V_0}}| > |\frac{A-B}{2V_0}|).$$

To show that formulae (2.14) and (2.15) correspond exactly to the formulae for the new index numbers given at the outset of this paper, it remains to be proved that $L-\Lambda=(A-B)/V_0$. This proof can easily be rendered by replacing V_0^i by $Q_0^iP_0^i$, q_n^i by Q_n^i/Q_0^i, and p_n^i by P_n^i/P_0^i in the expressions for A and B implied in formulae (2.7) and (2.8). This results in

$$(2.16)\quad A=\tfrac{1}{2}\sum_i Q_0^iP_0^i(\frac{P_n^i}{P_0^i}+1)(\frac{Q_n^i}{Q_0^i}-1)=\tfrac{1}{2}\sum_i (P_n^i+P_0^i)(Q_n^i-Q_0^i)$$

and

$$(2.17)\quad B = \tfrac{1}{2}\sum_i (Q_n^i+Q_0^i)(P_n^i-P_0^i).$$

Substitution of (2.16) and (2.17) in the expression $(A-B)/V_0$ results in

$$\frac{A-B}{V_0} = \frac{\sum_i(P_n^i+P_0^i)(Q_n^i-Q_0^i)-\sum_i(Q_n^i+Q_0^i)(P_n^i-P_0^i)}{2\sum_i P_0^iQ_0^i} =$$

$$(2.18)\quad = \frac{\sum_i P_0^iQ_n^i}{\sum_i P_0^iQ_0^i} - \frac{\sum_i Q_0^iP_n^i}{\sum_i Q_0^iP_0^i} = L - \Lambda$$

which is what had to be proved."

Following the above derivation, Stuvel [24] discusses some of the properties of these indexes. The interested reader may refer to his original paper.

CHAPTER THREE

FACTORIAL APPROACH

3.0 Chapter Summary: In this chapter, we provide the rationale of the "factorial approach," and develop the necessary calculus needed to construct the "True Index" of Cost of Living (the Economic Price Index) and the "True Index" of quantity (the Economic Quantity Index). Most of this presentation is a review of earlier work, except for some technical details which are brought in to spell out and strengthen the estimation procedure. The last section contains a statistical table which is intended to show how the National Income of a country may be split into two independent components, one due to price and the other due to quantity (or output). The same National Income data are utilized to illustrate the numerical calculations of the "True Index" of Cost of Living, (Economic Price Index) and the Economic Quantity Index as such data show the same types of expenditure totals which are required for these calculations.

3.1 A 2^2-Factorial Experiment in a Randomized Block Design: We start with the well-known model,

$$(3.1) \qquad y_{ij} = \mu + \alpha_i + \beta_j + \alpha\beta_{ij} + \varepsilon_{ij},$$

which characterizes a 2^2-factorial experiment arranged in a randomized block design with one replication, where y_{ij} = the response of the ith level (i=0,1) of the first factor (say, a) and jth level (j=0,1) of the second factor (say, b), μ = the general effect, α_i = the effect of the ith level of the factor a, β_j = the effect of the jth level of the factor b, $\alpha\beta_{ij}$ = the interaction effect of the ith level of a on the jth level of b, ε_{ij} = the random error (due to uncontrollable causes or factors). The usual constraints, admitted in design of experiments, are $\Sigma\alpha_i = \Sigma\beta_j = \sum_i \alpha\beta_{ij} = \sum_j \alpha\beta_{ij} = 0$. The responses, y_{00}, y_{10}, y_{01} and y_{11}, are conventionally denoted by

a_0b_0, a_1b_0, a_0b_1, and a_1b_1, or equivalently by 1, a, b and ab (the presence of a letter denoting the presence of the factor at level 1 and the absence denoting the level 0 of the factor).

It is well known that the "least squares" (Gauss-Markoff) estimates of the mean μ, the main effect A and B, and the interaction AB are given by

$$\begin{aligned}
\mu &= \tfrac{1}{4}(y_{00}+y_{10}+y_{01}+y_{11}) = \tfrac{1}{4}(1+a+b+ab) = \tfrac{1}{4}[(a+1)(b+1)] \\
A &= \tfrac{1}{2}(-y_{00}+y_{10}-y_{01}+y_{11}) = \tfrac{1}{2}(-1+a-b+ab) = \tfrac{1}{2}[(a-1)(b+1)] \\
B &= \tfrac{1}{2}(-y_{00}-y_{10}+y_{01}+y_{11}) = \tfrac{1}{2}(-1-a-b+ab) = \tfrac{1}{2}[(a+1)(b-1)] \\
AB &= \tfrac{1}{2}(y_{00}-y_{10}-y_{01}+y_{11}) = \tfrac{1}{2}(1-a-b+ab) = \tfrac{1}{2}[(a-1)(b-1)].
\end{aligned} \tag{3.2}$$

The above least squares analysis is conventionally summarized in the following schematic form:

$$\begin{matrix} \text{Effect} \\ \begin{bmatrix} \text{Mean} \\ A \\ B \\ AB \end{bmatrix} \end{matrix} = \begin{matrix} \begin{matrix} 1 & a & b & ab \end{matrix} \\ \begin{bmatrix} +1 & +1 & +1 & +1 \\ -1 & +1 & -1 & +1 \\ -1 & -1 & +1 & +1 \\ +1 & -1 & -1 & +1 \end{bmatrix} \end{matrix} \tag{3.3}$$

The above scheme of signs (A Hadamard matrix of order 4 with orthogonal rows and columns) shows with what sign a factorial combination of the two factors will appear in a main effect or the interaction. Conversely, it also shows with what sign a main effect or the interaction will enter into the expression denoting a factorial combination. For example, $ab=\text{Mean}+\frac{1}{2}(A+B+AB)$, $A=\frac{1}{2}(-1+a-b+ab)$, etc.

3.2 <u>Use of the Factorial Approach and the Different Index Number Formulae</u>: The above least squares technique was applied in [3,4] to provide the price index, the quantity index and the "true index" of cost of living. The two factors are price (p) and quantity (q) and the levels are 0 and 1, the base period and the period of comparison, respectively. Corresponding to y_{00}, y_{10}, y_{01}, and y_{11}, we have the factorial combinations p_0q_0, p_1q_0, p_0q_1, and p_1q_1, which are abbreviated as 1, p, q, and pq. Instead of working with p_0q_0, p_1q_0, p_0q_1, and p_1q_1, we would work with the totals of expenditure over "n" commodities, Σp_0q_0, Σp_1q_0, Σp_0q_1, and Σp_1q_1. One could also work with the averages $\Sigma p_0q_0/n$, $\Sigma p_1q_0/n$, $\Sigma p_0q_1/n$ and $\Sigma p_1q_1/n$. This "n" corresponds to the "number of replications" in the terminology of Design of Experiments. Working with totals or their averages would make no difference, as in the estimating equations to follow, n, appearing on both sides as a divisor will cancel out.

At this point, an assumption was made following Divisia indexes, permitting Σpq to be expressed as the product P^*Q^*, where P^* represents a general price level and Q^* represents a measure of the physical volume of goods. This assumption would give the following identities:

$$(3.4) \qquad \begin{aligned} \Sigma p_0q_0 &= P_0^*Q_0^* , & \Sigma p_1q_0 &= P_1^*Q_0^* \\ \Sigma p_0q_1 &= P_0^*Q_1^* , & \Sigma p_1q_1 &= P_1^*Q_1^* . \end{aligned}$$

In this set-up, P_1^*/P_0^* and Q_1^*/Q_0^* represent respectively the price index π and the quantity index κ. (See Stuvel [24] and Banerjee [3,4]).

With the above orientation, it is possible to express the general mean, the main effects P, Q, and the interaction PQ in the following forms:

$$(3.5.1) \quad \text{Mean} = \frac{\Sigma p_0q_0+\Sigma p_1q_0+\Sigma p_0q_1+\Sigma p_1q_1}{4} = \frac{(P_1^*+P_0^*)(Q_1^*+Q_0^*)}{4} = \frac{V_0(\pi+1)(\kappa+1)}{4}$$

$$(3.5.2) \quad P = \frac{-\Sigma p_0q_0+\Sigma p_1q_0-\Sigma p_0q_1+\Sigma p_1q_1}{2} = \frac{(P_1^*-P_0^*)(Q_1^*+Q_0^*)}{2} = \frac{V_0(\pi-1)(\kappa+1)}{2}$$

(3.5.3) $$Q = \frac{-\Sigma p_0 q_0 - \Sigma p_1 q_0 + \Sigma p_0 q_1 + \Sigma p_1 q_1}{2} = \frac{(P_1^* + P_0^*)(Q_1^* - Q_0^*)}{2}$$

$$= \frac{V_0(\pi+1)(\kappa-1)}{2}$$

(3.5.4) $$PQ = \frac{\Sigma p_0 q_0 - \Sigma p_1 q_0 - \Sigma p_0 q_1 + \Sigma p_1 q_1}{2} = \frac{(P_1^* - P_0^*)(Q_1^* - Q_0^*)}{2}$$

$$= \frac{V_0(\pi-1)(\kappa-1)}{2} .$$

It may be observed here that equations (3.5.2) and (3.5.3) are the same as given by Stuvel's (2.9). It appears, however, that the validity and the implications of equations (2.9) could perhaps be more easily comprehended if the formulation of the equations were approached through the identities (3.4).

It was pointed out in [4] that any pair of the four identities, (3.5.1)-(3.5.4), would provide, when solved for π and κ, the price and the quantity indexes. Of the six possible pairs, the one with {(3.5.2,(3.5.3)} should be the most meaningful, as the solutions depend upon the price effect and the quantity effect. As pointed out in [4], the solutions from the other pairs, except from the pair, {(3.5.1),(3.5.4)}, are also interesting. That the solutions from the pair, {(3.5.1),(3.5.4)}, will be unrealistic should be intuitively clear from the fact that this pair depends only upon the general effect and the interaction. (The meaning of interaction in terms of the standards of living is spelled out in Section (3.7). The "general effect" may be interpreted as what is due to "subsistence" necessities).

The solutions from {(3.5.2),(3.5.3)} give the following price and quantity indexes,

$$\pi = \frac{L_p - L_q}{2} + \sqrt{\left(\frac{L_p - L_q}{2}\right)^2 + V_1/V_0}$$

(3.6)

$$\kappa = \frac{L_q - L_p}{2} + \sqrt{\left(\frac{L_q - L_p}{2}\right)^2 + V_1/V_0} \quad ,$$

where L_p and L_q are, respectively, Laspeyres indexes for price and quantity, and $V_0 = \Sigma p_0 q_0$, $V_1 = \Sigma p_1 q_1$. The indexes π and κ satisfy certain fundamental tests such as the time reversal and the factor reversal tests, and are, therefore, preferred to other known formulae. π is ideally suited as a "deflator." (For other properties of these indexes, see Stuvel [24] and Banerjee [3,4]).

The pair with equations, {(3.5.2),(3.5.4)}, which recognises the existence of the effect of price and the interaction, give the price and quantity indexes as:

(3.7)

$$\text{Price index} = L_p$$

$$\text{Quantity index} = \frac{V_1/V_0 - L_q}{L_p - 1} \quad .$$

Again, the equations with {(3.5.3),(3.5.4)} lead to the following indexes for price and quantity:

(3.8)

$$\text{Price index} = \frac{V_1/V_0 - L_p}{L_q - 1} \quad ,$$

$$\text{Quantity index} = L_q .$$

The limitation of the indexes in (3.7) and (3.8) lies not only in the fact that they do not satisfy the time reversal and factor reversal tests, but also in the fact that they are obtained from equations that admit of the existence of P and PQ, and of Q and PQ respectively, that is, of one main effect and the interaction in each case.

Similarly, the solutions from the pair of equations, {(3.5.1,(3.5.2)}, would provide the indexes as follows:

(3.9)

$$\text{Price index: } \frac{\Sigma p_1 (q_0 + q_1)}{\Sigma p_0 (q_0 + q_1)}$$

(3.10) Quantity Index: L_q.

Also, the price and the quantity indexes from the pair of equations {(3.5.1), (3.5.3)}, are obtained as

(3.11) Price Index: L_p

(3.12) Quantity Index: $\dfrac{\Sigma q_1(p_0+p_1)}{\Sigma q_0(p_0+p_1)}$.

This approach thus lends a new interpretation to Laspeyres' price and quantity indexes. We also notice that (3.9) and (3.12) are the well-known Edgeworth-Marshall indexes.

It may be noted that we have $V_1-V_0=P+Q$. That is, the value change comes out as the sum of two independent components, the effect of price and the effect of quantity. This property appears to be inherent in the Divisia Indexes (See equation (6.1) of Samuelson and Swamy [20]). This result is utilized later, in the sequel, to split National Income into the price component and the quantity component.

3.3 <u>Formulation for the True Index</u>: An indifference - defined price index denotes the ratio of (minimum) expenditures between two price situations ensuring the same standard of living. If two points in two situations on an indifference map are equivalent, the quantity index between such a pair of points should be unity. Conversely, if the quantity index between any two points is equal to unity, it would imply that the standards of living corresponding to the two points in the two situations are the same. If, therefore, a quantity q_1 in the situation 1 could be found (by any formulation) such that the quantity index κ between q_0 and q_1 is unity, then q_1 could be regarded as equivalent to q_0. The price index, π, found from such a formulation, will represent the "true index" of cost of living of the period 1 compared to the period 0.

As one illustration of this formulation, we may consider Fisher's ideal formulae for price and quantity, given by

$$F_p = \sqrt{\frac{V_{10}}{V_{00}}\frac{V_{11}}{V_{01}}}$$

$$F_q = \sqrt{\frac{V_{01}}{V_{00}}\frac{V_{11}}{V_{10}}} \quad ,$$

where $V_{jk} = \sum_{i=1}^{n} p_j^i q_k^i$ (j, k=0,1), is the cost of $q_k^i=(q_k^1,q_k^2,\ldots q_k^n)$ calculated at prices $p_j^i=(p_j^1,p_j^2,\ldots,p_j^n)$; F_p and F_q are Fisher's ideal indexes for price and quantity respectively. If not we set $F_q=1$, the price index reduces to V_{11}/V_{00}.

The condition $F_q=1$ implies that

$$V_{11}\, V_{01} = V_{10}\, V_{00} \;,$$

a condition which is provided by Frisch [13] in his double-expenditure method.

The condition of equivalence in our formulation can be worked out by equating the quantity index, κ, to unity. If this were done, i.e. if κ were set equal to unity in (3.5.3), it would follow from (3.5.3) that the "effect of quantity" is zero, that is,

$$\Sigma p_1 q_1 - \Sigma p_1 q_0 + \Sigma p_0 q_1 - \Sigma p_0 q_0 = 0$$

Or

(3.13) $$V_{11} - V_{10} + V_{01} - V_{00} = 0$$

If we set $\kappa=1$ in (3.5.2), we get

(3.14) $$\pi = \frac{V_{11}}{V_{00}} \;.$$

Thus, (3.13) provides the condition for finding the "true index." If q_1 is equivalent to q_0, then the corresponding "price index" should be given by (3.14), that is, by the ratio of the two expenditures in the two situations.

Condition (3.13) is similar to the condition worked out by Frisch [13] in his double-expenditure method. Multiplication there takes the place of addition in (3.13).

3.4 <u>Limits of the True Index of Cost of Living Obtained from the Factorial Approach</u>: The "true index" given by Konüs [17] lies within the limits of Laspeyres' price index, L_p, and Paasche's price index, P_p. Wald's index [26] also lies between similar limits. It is shown below that the true index, obtained from the factorial approach, also lies between L_p and P_p [9]. From (3.13) we have

$$V_{11} - V_{00} L_p + \frac{V_{11}}{P_p} - V_{00} = 0$$

From the above, we have

$$\frac{V_{11}}{V_{00}} = \frac{P_p(L_p + 1)}{P_p + 1} \tag{3.15}$$

The above gives the expression of the "true index" in terms of L_p and P_p.

Following Konüs, let us make two possible hypotheses. First, let us suppose $V_{10} > V_{11}$. Then, from (3.13), $V_{01} > V_{00}$. This implies

$$\frac{V_{10}}{V_{00}} > \frac{V_{11}}{V_{01}}, \text{ i.e., } L_p > P_p$$

If $L_p > P_p$, from (3.15),

$$\frac{V_{11}}{V_{00}} > P_p$$

Again, since $V_{10} > V_{11}$,

$$\frac{V_{10}}{V_{00}} > \frac{V_{11}}{V_{00}}, \text{ i.e., } L_p > \frac{V_{11}}{V_{00}}$$

Thus,

$$L_p > \frac{V_{11}}{V_{00}} > P_p \tag{3.16}$$

Let us now suppose the opposite, i.e., let $V_{10} < V_{11}$. Then, from (3.13), $V_{01} < V_{00}$. This implies

$$\frac{V_{10}}{V_{00}} < \frac{V_{11}}{V_{01}}, \text{ i.e., } L_p < P_p$$

If $L_p < P_p$, from (3.15),

$$\frac{V_{11}}{V_{00}} < P_p$$

Since $V_{10} < V_{11}$,

$$\frac{V_{10}}{V_{00}} < \frac{V_{11}}{V_{00}}, \text{ i.e., } L_p < \frac{V_{11}}{V_{00}}$$

Thus,

$$L_p < \frac{V_{11}}{V_{00}} < P_p \tag{3.17}$$

Hence, combining (3.16) and (3.17), we have

$$L_p \overset{>}{<} \frac{V_{11}}{V_{00}} \overset{>}{<} P_p$$

3.5 <u>True Index of Quantity (Economic Quantity Index)</u>: It may be observed here that from the same formulation the "true index" of quantity (Economic Quantity Index) may similarly be obtained. It has the form,

$$\frac{P_q(L_q + 1)}{(P_q + 1)} \; . \tag{3.18}$$

If we put $\pi=1$ in (3.5.2), the "true index" of quantity is obtained as $\kappa=V_{11}/V_{00}$. The defining condition coming from (3.5.2), is given by

$$V_{11} - V_{01} + V_{10} - V_{00} = 0 \tag{3.19}$$

Expression (3.18) is obtained from (3.19) and is similar to (3.15) in form. Laspeyres' and Paasche's price indexes in (3.15) are substituted by the corresponding quantity indexes in (3.18). The "true index" of quantity lies between L_q and P_q.

3.6 <u>The New Index of Cost of Living Compared with Those of Wald and Frisch</u>: The index (3.14), computed from the defining condition, can now be compared with those given by Wald [26] and Frisch (See [26] for the derivation).

Suppose the Engel curves C_0 and C_1 are linear and are given by the following equations:

$$C_0:\quad q_0^i = \alpha_0^i V + \beta_0^i$$

$$C_1:\quad q_1^i = \alpha_1^i V + \beta_1^i$$

$$(i = 1, 2, \ldots, n)$$

Let

$$\sum_{i=1}^{n} \alpha_j^i p_k^i = a_{jk} \text{ and } \sum_{i}^{n} \beta_j^i p_k^i = b_{jk}, \ (j, k=0,1)$$

Then,

$$a_{jj} = 1, \ b_{jj} = 0 \ (j=0,1).$$

Also,

$$\sum_{i=1}^{n} p_0^i q_0^i = V_{00}, \ V_{01} = a_{10} V_{11} + b_{10}, \ V_{10} = a_{01} V_{00} + b_{01}.$$

In terms of the above coefficients, Frisch's index as calculated by Wald [26], is given by

$$F = \frac{-b_{10} + \sqrt{b_{10}^2 + 4a_{10}a_{01}V_{00}^2 + 4a_{10}b_{01}V_{00}}}{2a_{10}\ V_{00}}$$

and, Wald's true index as calculated by Wald [26], is given by

$$W = \sqrt{\frac{a_{01}}{a_{10}}} + \frac{1}{V_{00}} \ \frac{b_{01} - \frac{b_{10}}{a_{10}} \sqrt{a_{01}a_{10}}}{1 + \sqrt{a_{10}a_{01}}},$$

while our index, obtained through the condition of equivalence (3.13), is obtained as

$$B = \frac{1+a_{01}}{1+a_{10}} + \frac{1}{V_{00}} \ \frac{(b_{01}-b_{10})}{1+a_{10}}.$$

The above formulae are based on linear Engel Curves and are therefore restricted. Form of formula (3.15), which does not depend upon linearity of the Engel curves, is more general.

3.7 <u>Interpretation of Factorial Effects and the Interaction</u>: It is known that $\Sigma p_1 q_0$ represents a higher standard of living than $\Sigma p_0 q_0$, in moving from the price situation 0 to the price situation 1, and that $\Sigma p_0 q_1$ represents a higher standard of living than $\Sigma p_1 q_1$ in moving from the price situation 1 to the price situation 0. It is assumed that the person (or the "class" of persons) in situation 0 has the same "taste" as that of the person (or the "class" of persons) in situation 1. Hence, the change in the standards, influenced by price, considering the situation 0, in the price direction 0→1, is $\Sigma p_1 q_0 - \Sigma p_0 q_0$. Similarly, the change in the standards, influenced by price, considering the situation 1, in the price direction 1→0, is $\Sigma p_0 q_1 - \Sigma p_1 q_1$, which, in the price direction 0→1, is $-[\Sigma p_0 q_1 - \Sigma p_1 q_1] = \Sigma p_1 q_1 - \Sigma p_0 q_1$. Thus, the average change in the standards in the price direction 0→1 is given by $\frac{1}{2}(-\Sigma p_0 q_0 + \Sigma p_1 q_0 - \Sigma p_0 q_1 + \Sigma p_1 q_1)$. This is what is obtained as P, the effect of price under the least squares approach. Similarly, the change in the standards, influenced by quantity, considering the situation 0, in the quantity direction 0→1, is $(\Sigma p_0 q_1 - \Sigma p_0 q_0)$, and the change in the standards, considering the situation 1, influenced by quantity, in the quantity direction 0→1, is $(\Sigma p_1 q_1 - \Sigma p_1 q_0)$. The average of the two is what is obtained as Q, the effect of quantity under the least squares approach (see also Stuvel [24]).

If the change in the standards influenced by price, considering the situation 0, is, by magnitude, the same as the change in the standards, influenced by price, considering the situation 1, then there is no "interaction" between price and quantity. In other words, the interaction, if any, is measured by their difference, that is, by $(\Sigma p_1q_1-\Sigma p_0q_1)$ - $(\Sigma p_1q_0-\Sigma p_0q_0)$ = $(\Sigma p_0q_0-\Sigma p_1q_0$ - $\Sigma p_0q_1+\Sigma p_1q_1)$. Since, this represents some sort of an average of two differences, a dividing factor of 2 is introduced (by convention as is adopted in agro-biological experiments, and which is consistent with scheme (3.3)). This is what is obtained as the interaction PQ under the least squares technique. It is thus noticed that the interaction PQ gives a measure of the difference between the differences of the two standards. This is obtained going by way of price change. Since the definition of interaction PQ is symmetrical with respect to both price and quantity, the same expression for PQ is obtained going by way of quantity change.

3.8 <u>A Modified Least Squares Model for Approximating the True Index of Cost of Living</u>: If the component of the "general effect" and the component of the "interaction" are dropped from model (3.1), the modified model will look like

$$(3.20)\qquad \begin{bmatrix}\Sigma p_0q_0\\ \Sigma p_1q_0\\ \Sigma p_0q_1\\ \Sigma p_1q_1\end{bmatrix} = \begin{matrix} \mathcal{P}_0 & \mathcal{P}_1 & \mathcal{Q}_1 & \mathcal{Q}_0 \\ \end{matrix} \begin{bmatrix}1 & 0 & 0 & 1\\ 0 & 1 & 0 & 1\\ 1 & 0 & 1 & 0\\ 0 & 1 & 1 & 0\end{bmatrix} + \begin{bmatrix}\varepsilon_{00}\\ \varepsilon_{10}\\ \varepsilon_{01}\\ \varepsilon_{11}\end{bmatrix},$$

where $\mathcal{P}_0$, $\mathcal{P}_1$, $\mathcal{Q}_1$, $\mathcal{Q}_0$ represent the effects of price and quantity at the respective levels with meanings similar to α_0, α_1, β_1, β_0 of model (3.1).

In model (3.20), we do not have to make the usual assumptions of Design of Experiments as was made for model (3.1) in the form $\Sigma\alpha_i=\Sigma\beta_j=\sum_i\alpha\beta_{ij}=\sum_j\alpha\beta_{ij} = 0$. Additivity is the only assumption. The associated design matrix X is singular. The rank of X = 3. The least squares estimate of the vector $\underline{\beta}' = [\mathcal{P}_0, \mathcal{P}_1, \mathcal{Q}_1, \mathcal{Q}_0]$, is given by

$$\hat{\underline{\beta}} = S^{-}X'\underline{Y}$$

where S^- is a pseudo-inverse of $S = [X'X]$, such that $S S^- S = S$. Such a pseudo-inverse exists. In such situations, $\underline{\beta}$ is not uniquely estimable. However, a linear function of the parameters, $\underline{\lambda}'\underline{\beta}$, is uniquely estimable, if and only if $\underline{\lambda}'H = \underline{\lambda}'$, where $\underline{\lambda}$ is a p×1 vector of constants, and $H = S^-S$. The estimate $\hat{\underline{\beta}}$ is indicated below along with $S = [X'X]$, S^- and H:

$$S=\begin{bmatrix} 2 & 0 & 1 & 1 \\ 0 & 2 & 1 & 1 \\ 1 & 1 & 2 & 0 \\ 1 & 1 & 0 & 2 \end{bmatrix}, \quad S^-=\begin{bmatrix} \frac{3}{4} & \frac{1}{4} & -\frac{1}{2} & 0 \\ \frac{1}{4} & \frac{3}{4} & -\frac{1}{2} & 0 \\ -\frac{1}{2} & -\frac{1}{2} & 1 & 0 \\ -1 & -1 & 1 & 0 \end{bmatrix}, \quad S^-S=H=\begin{bmatrix} 1 & 0 & 0 & 1 \\ 0 & 1 & 0 & 1 \\ 0 & 0 & 1 & -1 \\ 0 & 0 & 0 & 0 \end{bmatrix}$$

$$\hat{\underline{\beta}}=\begin{bmatrix} \hat{P}_0 \\ \hat{P}_1 \\ \hat{Q}_1 \\ \hat{Q}_0 \end{bmatrix} = \begin{bmatrix} \frac{3}{4}(\Sigma p_0q_0+\Sigma p_0q_1)+\frac{1}{4}(\Sigma p_1q_0+\Sigma p_1q_1)-\frac{1}{2}(\Sigma p_0q_1+\Sigma p_1q_1) \\ \frac{1}{4}(\Sigma p_0q_0+\Sigma p_0q_1)+\frac{3}{4}(\Sigma p_1q_0+\Sigma p_1q_1)-\frac{1}{2}(\Sigma p_0q_1+\Sigma p_1q_1) \\ -\frac{1}{2}(\Sigma p_0q_1+\Sigma p_0q_1)-\frac{1}{2}(\Sigma p_1q_0+\Sigma p_1q_1)+\frac{1}{2}(\Sigma p_0q_1+\Sigma p_1q_1) \\ 0 \end{bmatrix}$$

It can be easily verified that $\lambda_1'=[-1,1,0,0]$ and $\lambda_2'=[0,0,1,-1]$ satisfy the condition $\underline{\lambda}'H = \underline{\lambda}'$, and, therefore, $\underline{\lambda}_1'\underline{\beta}$ and $\underline{\lambda}_2'\underline{\beta}$ are both uniquely estimable. $\lambda_1'\hat{\beta}$ and $\lambda_2'\hat{\beta}$ represent respectively the estimated effect of price and the estimated effect of quantity, being given by

$$P=\hat{P}_1-\hat{P}_0=\frac{1}{2}(-\Sigma p_0q_0+\Sigma p_1q_0-\Sigma p_0q_1+\Sigma p_1q_1)$$

$$Q=\hat{Q}_1-\hat{Q}_0=\frac{1}{2}(-\Sigma p_0q_0-\Sigma p_1q_0+\Sigma p_0q_1+\Sigma p_1q_1) .$$

These estimates are the same as obtained before, and, therefore, the price index, the quantity index and the "true index" of cost of living remain the same.

To estimate $\underline{\beta}$, we could also use the Moore-Penrose unique g-inverse $S^{\dagger}$ for S^{-}, where $S^{\dagger}$ is such that (i) $S S^{\dagger} S = S$, (ii) $S^{\dagger} S S^{\dagger} = S^{\dagger}$, (iii) $(S S^{\dagger})' = S S^{\dagger}$ and (iv) $(S^{\dagger} S)' = S^{\dagger} S$. If S^{-} is substituted by $S^{\dagger}$, the estimate of $\underline{\beta}$ is obtained as $\underline{\tilde{\beta}} = X^{\dagger} Y$. The estimator $\underline{\tilde{\beta}}$ is different from $\underline{\hat{\beta}}$, and is such that the norm $||\underline{X}\beta - \underline{Y}||$ is minimum for all $\underline{\beta}$. If $\underline{\lambda}'\underline{\hat{\beta}}$ is unique, the same unique value will be the value of $\underline{\lambda}'\underline{\tilde{\beta}}$. In this setting, the estimate of $\underline{\beta}' = [P_0, P_1, Q_1, Q_0]$ is obtained as follows:

$$\underline{\tilde{\beta}} \quad \begin{bmatrix} \tilde{P}_0 \\ \tilde{P}_1 \\ \tilde{Q}_1 \\ \tilde{Q}_0 \end{bmatrix} = X^{\dagger} \begin{bmatrix} \Sigma p_0 q_0 \\ \Sigma p_1 q_0 \\ \Sigma p_0 q_1 \\ \Sigma p_1 q_1 \end{bmatrix} = \frac{1}{8} \begin{bmatrix} 3 & -1 & 3 & -1 \\ -1 & 3 & -1 & 3 \\ -1 & -1 & 3 & 3 \\ 3 & 3 & -1 & -1 \end{bmatrix} \begin{bmatrix} \Sigma p_0 q_0 \\ \Sigma p_1 q_0 \\ \Sigma p_0 q_1 \\ \Sigma p_1 q_1 \end{bmatrix}$$

$$(3.21) = \frac{1}{8} \begin{bmatrix} 3\Sigma p_0 q_0 - \Sigma p_1 q_0 + 3\Sigma p_0 q_1 - \Sigma p_1 q_1 \\ -\Sigma p_0 q_0 + 3\Sigma p_1 q_0 - \Sigma p_0 q_1 + 3\Sigma p_1 q_1 \\ -\Sigma p_0 q_0 - \Sigma p_1 q_0 + 3\Sigma p_0 q_1 + 3\Sigma p_1 q_1 \\ 3\Sigma p_0 q_0 + 3\Sigma p_1 q_0 - \Sigma p_0 q_1 - \Sigma p_1 q_1 \end{bmatrix} .$$

Here, again, $\underline{\lambda}_1'\underline{\beta}$ and $\underline{\lambda}_2'\underline{\beta}$ are both uniquely estimable, providing the same unique estimates of the main effects of price and quantity in the same forms, thus furnishing the same indexes. The verification is simple.

It may be of interest to observe that the estimates in (3.21) are such that the price index π and the quantity index κ from $(\tilde{P}_0, \tilde{P}_1)$ and from $(\tilde{Q}_0, \tilde{Q}_1)$ are easily verified to be the same as obtained from {(3.5.1), (3.5.2)} and {(3.5.1, (3.5.3)} respectively.

The above analyses were not perhaps necessary in view of the fact that the four equations, (3.5.1)-(3.5.4), emerge from four mutually <u>orthogonal</u> components, and, therefore, dropping the parameters the way we have done would not alter the estimates of the price effect and the quantity effect.

3.9 Price and Quantity Components in Value Change of National Income: In this section, we consider a practical situation in which the above formulae are applied to explain value changes in terms of price and quantity variations. "True index" of cost of living and the "true index" of quantity are also numerically illustrated, although the data may not be quite relevant for such a study.

Estimates of national income are available for Indian Union in the publications entitled, "Estimates of National Income," published by the Central Statistical Organization. These papers show a statement on the movement of net national output at factor cost from year to year. Comparison of the national output is made possible, as usual, through the indexes of national output provided at current prices (indexes of value) and constant prices (indexes of output or quantity). These indexes furnish, of course, a basis of comparison over the years, but a complete picture of the movement of national income will not be available unless it is known how much of the change in value is due to change in price and how much to change in output (quantity).

In "Estimates of National Income," the values of L_q (quantity index) and V_{11}/V_{00} (value index) are provided, but not the values of L_p (price index). For L_p (Laspeyres' price index), we take the wholesale price indexes[4] for India as close substitutes. These price indexes (base 1939=100) are not, of course, identical with the price indexes which would have been obtained from the statistics utilized in the estimation of national income. However, the order of disagreement between the two is probably not so large as to vitiate the study to an unacceptable

---

[4]Vide reports issued by the Office of the Economic Adviser, Government of India.

extent, or to make the computations absolutely hypothetical.

The computed price components and quantity components in value change are given in the following Table for the period 1949-50 to 1957-58.

In Table 1, the values of L_q (Col. 3) and V_{11}/V_{00} (Col. 4) are taken from the papers on national income, while, the values of L_p (Col. 2), as stated before, are the whole-sale price indexes obtained as simple averages of the monthly indexes for 12 months of the corresponding fiscal years; π and κ (Cols. 6 and 7 respectively) are the adjusted price and quantity indexes. Column 5 shows the percentage change of value of net national output as given by

$$100\left(\frac{V_{11}}{V_{00}} - 1\right).$$

The percentage difference as shown in Col. 5 is obviously the sum of the components in Cols. 8 and 9.

Table 1 shows that during the years, 1954-55 and 1955-56, the price component, that is, the contribution made by price to value change, has been negative, as the corresponding price index (adjusted) is less than 100. As a result, a part of the contribution made by quantity (output) to the increase in value of national income during those years has been masked by the depressing price effect. This table provides a complete picture.

Such a picture can be presented for the National Income of any country.

Paasche's price index P_p is calculated in Col. 10. Formula (3.15) is utilized to compute the "true index" of cost of living (economic price index) in Col. 11. It is noticed that the "true index" lies between L_p and P_p.

Again, Paasche's quantity index P_q is shown in Col. 12 and the "true index" of quantity in Col. 13 (from Formula (3.18)). The "true index" of quantity (economic quantity index) lies between L_q and P_q.

The above economic indices are calculated from these data for illustrative purposes only.

TABLE 1. PRICE AND QUANTITY COMPONENTS IN NATIONAL INCOME

years	L_p	L_q	$100(\frac{V_{11}}{V_{00}})$	$100(\frac{V_{11}}{V_{00}}-1)$	π	κ	P	Q	P_p	True Index of Cost of Living	P_q	True Index of Quantity
(1)	(2)	(3)	(4)	(5)	(6)	(7)	(8)	(9)	(10)	(11)	(12)	(13)
1948-49	100.0	100.0	100.0	0.0	100.0	100.0	0.0	0.0	100.0	100.0	100.0	100.0
-50	103.0	102.0	104.2	4.2	102.6	101.6	2.6	1.6	102.2	102.6	101.2	101.6
-51	109.6	102.3	110.2	10.2	108.7	101.4	8.7	1.5	107.7	108.7	100.5	101.4
-52	116.3	105.2	115.3	15.3	113.1	102.0	13.2	2.1	109.6	113.1	99.1	102.1
-53	101.8	109.4	113.5	13.5	102.8	110.4	3.0	10.5	103.8	102.8	111.5	110.4
-54	106.3	116.0	121.2	21.2	105.4	115.1	5.8	15.4	104.5	105.4	114.0	115.1
-55	101.0	118.8	111.1	11.1	96.4	114.2	-3.4	14.5	93.5	97.1	110.0	114.6
-56	96.4	121.2	115.4	15.4	95.7	120.5	-4.7	20.1	95.2	95.8	119.7	120.5
-57	107.1	127.2	130.8	30.8	104.8	124.9	5.3	25.5	102.8	105.0	122.1	124.9
-58	110.3	125.2	131.3	31.3	107.4	122.3	8.2	23.1	104.9	107.7	119.0	122.4

CHAPTER FOUR
MULTI DIMENSIONAL INDEXES PROVIDED BY THE FACTORIAL APPROACH

4.0 Chapter Summary: It is shown in this chapter how "index numbers" can be constructed and used for expressions for the main effects in case of 2^n-factorial experiments. Such indexes satisfy the tests basic in the theory of index numbers and are easy to calculate. The factorial combinations which get involved in these indexes constitute a special kind of meaningful fractional replicates. As the fractions are small, such replicates may be conveniently used for experimental purposes, and index numbers readily constructed to indicate the trend of main effects. These index formulae may also be taken over to econometric fields for use as multi-dimensional indexes.

4.1 Introduction: In case of a 2^n-factorial experiment, when it is not possible for a large value of n, to have a full replicate, resort is made to a fractional plan which affords an evaluation, at least, of the more important effects. Depending upon the nature of the fractional replicate, some effects would come out as aliases of others, and some of the high order interactions would have to be ignored as being unimportant. For large values of n, it may be required at times to secure the smallest fraction of a full replicate so that at least all the main effects could be estimated without letting any of them be confounded with any other effect of importance. For such a design, the labor involved in the computations could be reduced considerably, if the main effects were evaluated in the manner discussed in this note.

4.2 Rationale of the New Approach: A main effect (or an interaction) is, as is well known, available as a difference or as an average of differences. An effect could perhaps be expressed just as well as a ratio. In case of one factor, say, p, at two levels, 1 and 0, its effect, P, is expressed as $P=(p_1-p_0)$. The same effect could also be expressed as a ratio as $\pi=p_1/p_0$. With two factors p and q at two levels each, there will be four factorial combinations, p_1q_1, p_1q_0, p_0q_1, and p_0q_0. If each of these treatment combinations were given to a series of plots (as in an agricultural experiment), the total yield from each of these combinations would be denoted by Σp_1q_1, Σp_1q_0, Σp_0q_1, and Σp_0q_0, respectively. These four totals would enter into the expressions for the two main effects and the interaction as an average of two differences in each case. One might also perhaps express the effect of the factor p as $\Sigma p_1q_0/\Sigma p_0q_0$, or as $\Sigma p_1q_1/\Sigma p_0q_1$ or perhaps as the geometric mean of the two, as $[(\Sigma p_1q_0/\Sigma p_0q_0)(\Sigma p_1q_1/\Sigma p_0q_1)]^{1/2}$. The effect of the second factor, q, could also be expressed similarly as ratios. It will easily be recognized that the first ratio resembles Laspeyres' index, the second, Paasche's, and the third, the ideal index of Fisher.

In case of three factors, p, q, r, each at 2 levels, 1 and 0, the effect of p, as an extension of the ideal formula of Fisher could perhaps be expressed as

$$[(\frac{\Sigma p_1q_0r_0}{\Sigma p_0q_0r_0})(\frac{\Sigma p_1q_1r_0}{\Sigma p_0q_1r_0})(\frac{\Sigma p_1q_0r_1}{\Sigma p_0q_0r_1})(\frac{\Sigma p_1q_1r_1}{\Sigma p_0q_1r_1})]^{1/4} .$$

Such indexes could be obtained for each of the three factors, p, q, and r to show the effects. Thus, for three factors, it would have been necessary to compute four different ratios and take the fourth root of their product. If, however, four factors were involved at two levels each, and if we proceeded as above, the index for a main effect could be obtained as the eighth root of the product of eight ratios.

The above is indicated not to recommend that we should calculate indexes in the above manner as expressions for the factorial effects, but is shown merely to suggest that use of index numbers as a ready method to express factorial effects will have a meaning in the field of factorial experimentation. If we proceeded in the manner as indicated above, we would have soon got involved in heavy calculations and thus lost the simplicity and also the elegance as is due to the usual procedure of analysis of 2^n-factorial experiments. It will be clear from the above that computational labor would increase with an increase in the number of factors. Again, apart from the computational labor, such formulae as indexes might not be advised, as these would not satisfy certain tests as are inherent in the theory of index numbers.

4.3 The Aim: What we aim at is to evolve standardized yet simple formulae through an approach which unifies the methodology of construction of index numbers as in economic fields with that of the usual procedure of analysis of factorial experiments. If we were interested in getting a tentative indication of only the main effects in case of a large number of factors, we would have perhaps thought of the smallest fractional replicate which would save at least the main effects. This requirement will be met by the present approach, where expressions for the main effects would come out in the shape of index numbers. The index number formulae will involve only $(2n+2)$ of the 2^n-factorial combinations, and the formulae will take standardized forms for any n. It will satisfy the "tests" inherent in the theory of Index Numbers, and yet be simple. As pointed out above, we need to make only $(2n+2)$ observations (or runs) out of a total of 2^n. The saving will increase with an increase in the value of n. A full replicate will, however, be necessary for n=2 and 3.

Such formulae could also be used as index number formulae in economic fields involving more than two factors, and might be called multi-dimensional indexes [22,27]. This approach incidentally establishes a new relationship between the theory of index numbers and fractional replicates of a special kind.

Such an approach as indicated in this note is just an alternative way of looking at factorial experiments, and, in this context, special mention may be made of the manner in which Bechhofer [10] looked at factorial experiments. Bechhofer suggested that multifactor experiments could be conducted to study factorial effects on the variance (and not on the mean response) of a chance variable and was that way led to adopt a multiplicative model [10] indicating relative changes just as index numbers would.

4.4 <u>The Approach</u>: The procedure will be illustrated here first with reference to two factors, and then extended to three. A hint will then be given for four factors. The methodology for four factors will be such as will readily suggest the way to generalization for any number of factors. Also, the symmetry in the index number formulae will clearly indicate what forms the formulae will assume in general for any number of factors.

Let there be two factors, p and q, each at two levels, 1 and 0. The main effects and the interaction as formally defined (see Chapters Two and Three) in the analysis of factorial experiments may be shown as given below:

$$P=\frac{1}{2}[p_1^iq_1^i-p_0^iq_1^i+p_1^iq_0^i-p_0^iq_0^i]=\frac{1}{2}(p_1^i-p_0^i)(q_1^i+q_0^i)$$
$$=\frac{1}{2}p_0^iq_0^i(\pi^i-1)(\kappa^i+1)$$

$$Q=\frac{1}{2}[p_1^iq_1^i+p_0^iq_1^i-p_1^iq_0^i-p_0^iq_0^i]=\frac{1}{2}(p_1^i+p_0^i)(q_1^i-q_0^i)$$
$$=\frac{1}{2}p_0^iq_0^i(\pi^i+1)(\kappa^i-1),$$

$$PQ=\frac{1}{2}[p_1^iq_1^i-p_0^iq_1^i-p_1^iq_0^i+p_0^iq_0^i]=\frac{1}{2}(p_1^i-p_0^i)(q_1^i-q_0^i)$$
$$=\frac{1}{2}p_0^iq_0^i(\pi^i-1)(\kappa^i-1),$$

where i refers to the i-th replication, $\pi^i=p_1^i/p_0^i$, $\kappa^i=q_1^i/q_0^i$, and each combination represents the corresponding yield from the plot given to it. For instance $p_1^iq_1^i$ or $p_1^iq_0^i$

would represent the yield obtained from the plot given to $p_1^i q_1^i$ or to $p_1^i q_0^i$, as the case may be, in the i-th replication.

In the above representation, the multiplying factor is $\frac{1}{2}$. In general, if there are n factors, the multiplying factor, as is well known, will be $(\frac{1}{2})^{n-1}$.

The main effects and the interaction can be conveniently represented in a schematic form as given below (vide scheme 3.3):

Effect	$p_0^i q_0^i$ $\equiv p_0^i q_0^i(1)$	$p_1^i q_0^i$ $\equiv p_0^i q_0^i(\pi^i)$	$p_0^i q_1^i$ $\equiv p_0^i q_0^i(\kappa^i)$	$p_1^i q_1^i$ $\equiv p_0^i q_0^i(\pi^i \kappa^i)$
Mean	+	+	+	+
P	-	+	-	+
Q	-	-	+	+
PQ	+	-	-	+

(4.1)

The above scheme shows with what sign a factorial combination of the two factors will appear in a main effect or in the interaction. Reversely, this also shows with what sign a main effect or the interaction will enter in a factorial combination. For example, $p_1^i q_1^i = \text{Mean} + \frac{1}{2}[P+Q+PQ]$.

It will be noticed that the above scheme of signs of + and - represents a 4×4 orthogonal matrix. This orthogonality of the matrix insures that the four components are independent.

The main effects and the interaction are shown below in terms of the differences of a few specific factorial combinations:

No.	Combination	Equivalent Expressions in Terms of Main Effects and the Interaction
(i)	$p_1^i q_1^i - p_0^i q_0^i$ $= V_0(\pi^i \kappa^i - 1)$	$P+Q=\frac{1}{2}V_0^i[(\pi^i-1)(\kappa^i+1)$ $+(\pi^i+1)(\kappa^i-1)]$
(ii)	$p_1^i q_1^i - p_0^i q_1^i$ $= V_0(\pi^i \kappa^i - \kappa^i)$	$P+PQ=\frac{1}{2}V_0^i[(\pi^i-1)(\kappa^i+1)$ $+(\pi^i-1)(\kappa^i-1)]$
(iii)	$p_1^i q_1^i - p_1^i q_0^i$ $= V_0^i(\pi^i \kappa^i - \pi^i)$	$Q+PQ=\frac{1}{2}V_0^i[(\pi^i+1)(\kappa^i-1)$ $+(\pi^i-1)(\kappa^i-1)]$

In the above, $V_0^i = p_0^i q_0^i$. Each of the three combinations, (i), (ii), and (iii), is the sum of two independent components. Let

$$V_1^i = p_1^i q_1^i .$$

Then, we have

$$(4.2)\quad \begin{aligned} V_1^i - V_0^i &= V_0^i\left(\frac{V_1^i}{V_0^i} - 1\right) = V_0^i(\pi^i \kappa^i - 1) = P+Q \\ &= \frac{V_0^i}{2}[(\pi^i-1)(\kappa^i+1)+(\pi^i+1)(\kappa^i-1)]. \end{aligned}$$

It is noticed that the difference, $(V_1^i - V_0^i)$, is composed of the two main effect components.

Stuvel [24] intuitively hit upon identity (4.2) in the form,

$$(4.3)\quad V_0^i(\pi^i \kappa^i - 1) = \frac{V_0^i}{2}(\pi^i+1)(\kappa^i-1) + \frac{V_0^i}{2}(\pi^i-1)(\kappa^i+1)$$

as an Arithmetic Average of the identities,

$$V_0^i(\pi^i \kappa^i - 1) = V_0^i[\pi^i(\kappa^i-1)+(\pi^i-1)]$$

and

$$V_0^i(\pi^i \kappa^i - 1) = V_0^i[\kappa^i(\pi^i-1)+(\kappa^i-1)]$$

and, from this identity, proceeded to work out the price index and the quantity index. Since (4.3) holds for each single commodity i (i refers to a replication in the present context), (4.3) may be summated over all the n commodities giving rise to

(4.4)
$$\sum_i V_1^i - \sum_i V_0^i = \sum_i \frac{V_0^i(\pi^i+1)(\kappa^i-1)}{2} + \sum_i \frac{V_0^i(\pi^i-1)(\kappa^i+1)}{2}$$
$$= \sum_i A^i + \sum_i B^i,$$

where

$$A^i \equiv \frac{V_0^i(\pi^i+1)(\kappa^i-1)}{2}, \quad B^i \equiv \frac{V_0^i(\pi^i-1)(\kappa^i+1)}{2}.$$

Equation (4.4) may be written as $V_1 - V_0 = A + B$, where

$$V_1 = \sum_i V_1^i, \quad V_0 \equiv \sum_i V_0^i, \quad A \equiv \sum_i A^i$$

and

$$B \equiv \sum_i B^i.$$

Each of the two components af (4.4) is a summation over i individual commodities, where π^i and κ^i are, respectively, the price and the quantity indexes for the i-th commodity. As we are interested in the over-all price index and the over-all quantity index covering all the i commodities, these could be obtained from the following equations [24], where the suffix i has been dropped off to cover all the i commodities. This generalization, effected through the dropping off of the suffix i, is tantamount to changing, as if, the running value of a variable to the variable itself. (The two equations which follow are based on two orthogonal components).

(4.5)
$$\frac{V_0(\pi+1)(\kappa-1)}{2} = A \text{ and}$$
$$\frac{V_0(\pi-1)(\kappa+1)}{2} = B.$$

A word seems to be in order in justification of the above type of generalization effected through the dropping of the suffix i. This, in effect, says that what holds for the value of a single commodity is made to hold good for the value of n commodities. Such a practice is prevalent in the theory of Index Numbers. Some of the "basic tests" which Index Numbers are expected to satisfy were developed from the corresponding properties of single commodities. However, in section (3.2) we developed these equations through a different approach.

In the above equations, π and κ represent the indexes for p and q. Eliminating π from the above, the equation in κ is obtained in the form (see Chapters Two and Three),

$$\kappa^2+\frac{B-A}{V_0}\kappa-V_1/V_0=0$$

and solves for κ as

$$\kappa=\frac{A-B}{2V_0}+\sqrt{\left(\frac{A-B}{2V_0}\right)^2+V_1/V_0},\quad \text{or}$$

as

$$\kappa=\frac{1}{2}\left(\frac{\Sigma p_0q_1}{\Sigma p_0q_0}-\frac{\Sigma p_1q_0}{\Sigma p_0q_0}\right)+\sqrt{\left\{\frac{1}{2}\left(\frac{\Sigma p_0q_1}{\Sigma p_0q_0}-\frac{\Sigma p_1q_0}{\Sigma p_0q_0}\right)\right\}^2+V_1/V_0}.$$

The other root is ruled out as this would give a negative value for the index. In the same manner, π is obtained as

$$\pi=\frac{1}{2}\left(\frac{\Sigma p_1q_0}{\Sigma p_0q_0}-\frac{\Sigma p_0q_1}{\Sigma p_0q_0}\right)+\sqrt{\left\{\frac{1}{2}\left(\frac{\Sigma p_1q_0}{\Sigma p_0q_0}-\frac{\Sigma p_0q_1}{\Sigma p_0q_0}\right)\right\}^2+V_1/V_0}.$$

The indexes, π and κ, satisfy certain fundamental tests, such as the "time reversal" and the "factor reversal" tests, and may, therefore, be preferred in practice to other known formulae, [24,6].

Price and quantity take the place of the two factors, expenditure that of yield and the periods 1 and 0 as the two levels in the context of our present discussion.

The required indexes for the main effects, P and Q, would thus be obtained as π and κ as above.

4.5 Notations: For the sake of simplicity, the following notations will be introduced. For two factors, Laspeyres' formulae will be denoted as

$$L_{p/q}=\Sigma p_1q_0/\Sigma p_0q_0.$$

For more than two factors, we shall write

$L_{p/qrs...}$ for $\Sigma p_1q_0r_0s_0.../\Sigma p_0q_0r_0s_0...$,

$L_{pq/rs...}$ for $\Sigma p_1q_1r_0s_0.../\Sigma p_0q_0r_0s_0...$,

etc.

For four factors, for instance, we shall write $L_{p/qrs}$ for $\Sigma p_1q_0r_0s_0/\Sigma p_0q_0r_0s_0$ and write $L_{qrs/p}$ for $\Sigma p_0q_1r_1s_1/\Sigma p_0q_0r_0s_0$.

Further, for two factors, as already stated,

$$V_1 \equiv \sum_i V_1^i=\sum_i p_1^iq_1^i, \quad V_0 \equiv \sum_i V_0^i=\sum_i p_0^iq_0^i.$$

The difference, $(V_1^i-V_0^i)$, shall be termed as amplitude and will be denoted as α_{pq}^i for two factors. Similarly, (V_1-V_0) will be denoted as α_{pq}, while the ratio V_1/V_0 as R_{pq} for two factors. For four factors, we shall write α_{pqrs}^i for $(p_1^iq_1^ir_1^is_1^i-p_0^iq_0^ir_0^is_0^i)$ and R_{pqrs} for $\sum_i p_1^iq_1^ir_1^is_1^i/\sum_i p_0^iq_0^ir_0^is_0^i$, and so on.

4.6 The Indexes for Three Factors: Let the third factor be 'r'. Then, corresponding to the 4×4 orthogonal matrix as in (1), we shall have an 8×8 orthogonal matrix to express schematically the main effects and the interactions of a 2^3-factorial experiment in terms of the different combinations and vice versa. For three factors, we shall have the amplitude as α_{pqr}^i=P+Q+R+PQR. It is to be noted that, in this case, the difference, $(p_1^iq_1^ir_1^i-p_0^iq_0^ir_0^i)$, comes out as the sum of the three main effects and the three-factor interaction. If, now, equations similar to (4.5) are obtained, we shall have

$$(4.6)\quad \begin{aligned} &\text{(i)} \quad \frac{V_0'}{4}(\pi-1)(\kappa+1)(\rho+1) = A' \\ &\text{(ii)} \quad \frac{V_0'}{4}(\pi+1)(\kappa-1)(\rho+1) = B' \\ &\text{(iii)} \quad \frac{V_0'}{4}(\pi+1)(\kappa+1)(\rho-1) = C' \\ &\text{(iv)} \quad \frac{V_0'}{4}(\pi-1)(\kappa-1)(\rho-1) = \delta'. \end{aligned}$$

where π, κ, and ρ are the indexes for the factors p, q, and r,

$$A'=\sum_i A^{i'}=\sum_i \frac{V_0^{i'}(\pi^i-1)(\kappa^i+1)(\rho^i+1)}{4}$$

$$B'=\sum_i B^{i'}=\sum_i \frac{V_0^{i'}(\pi^i+1)(\kappa^i-1)(\rho^i+1)}{4}$$

$$C'=\sum_i C^{i'}=\sum_i \frac{V_0^{i'}(\pi^i+1)(\kappa^i+1)(\rho^i-1)}{4}$$

$$\delta'=\sum_i \delta^{i}=\sum_i \frac{V_0^{i'}(\pi^i-1)(\kappa^i-1)(\rho^i-1)}{4}$$

$$\pi^i=p_1^i/p_0^i, \quad \kappa^i=q_1^i/q_0^i, \quad \rho^i=\frac{r_1^i}{r_0^i},$$

and

$V_0'=\sum_i V_0^{i'}=\sum_i p_0^i q_0^i r_0^i$, (a prime being placed above V_0 to distinguish it from V_0 used before).

In (4.6), there are four equations with three variables, π, κ, and ρ, whereas in (4.5), there were two equations with two variables π and κ. It was possible to have two equations with two variables in (4.5), because the amplitude, $\alpha_{pq}^i=(p_1^i q_1^i-p_0^i q_0^i)$, was expressible as the sum of two components P and Q which are the two main effects. But, in the present case, an additional component (the three-factor interaction), besides the three main-effect components, enters into the amplitude.

Higher order interactions are usually ignored. If, therefore, we could assume that the term corresponding to the three-factor interaction, δ', were zero, the equations could be easily solved.

To be consistent with the usual notations, we would write A'B'C' for δ'. From equations (4.6), we have

$$A'-B'-C'+A'B'C'=V_0'(\pi-\kappa\rho) \text{ or } A'-B'-C'=V_0'(\pi-\kappa\rho),$$

as A'B'C'=0. Three such equations may be obtained as follows:

$$(4.7)\qquad \begin{aligned} V_0'(\pi-\kappa\rho)&=A'-B'-C' \\ V_0'(\kappa-\rho\pi)&=B'-C'-A' \\ V_0'(\rho-\pi\kappa)&=C'-A'-B'. \end{aligned}$$

We further have

$$V_1'-V_0'=A'+B'+C'+A'B'C', \text{ and}$$

$$V_0'(\pi\kappa\rho-1)=A'+B'+C'+A'B'C',$$

where

$$V_1'=\sum_i p_1^i q_1^i r_1^i, \qquad V_0'=\sum_i p_0^i q_0^i r_0^i .$$

Hence,

$$(4.8)\qquad \pi\kappa\rho=V_1'/V_0'.$$

Solving the equations (4.7) with the help of the identity (4.8), we get

$$\pi=\frac{A'-(B'+C')}{2V_0'} + \sqrt{\left[\frac{A'-(B'+C')}{2V_0'}\right]^2+ V_1'/V_0'}$$

$$\kappa=\frac{B'-(C'+A')}{2V_0'} + \sqrt{\left[\frac{B'-(C'+A')}{2V_0'}\right]^2+ V_1'/V_0'}$$

$$\rho=\frac{C'-(A'+B')}{2V_0'} + \sqrt{\left[\frac{C'-(A'+B')}{2V_0'}\right]^2+ V_1'/V_0'} .$$

Remembering that the three-factor interaction

$$\sum_i \frac{(p_1^i-p_0^i)(q_1^i-q_0^i)(r_1^i-r_0^i)}{4} = 0,$$

we get the indexes for the three factors finally reduced to the forms,

$$\pi=\tfrac{1}{2}(L_{p/qr}-L_{qr/p})+\sqrt{[\tfrac{1}{2}(L_{p/qr}-L_{qr/p})]^2+R_{pqr}}\ ,$$

(4.9)
$$\kappa=\tfrac{1}{2}(L_{q/pr}-L_{pr/q})+\sqrt{[\tfrac{1}{2}(L_{q/pr}-L_{pr/q})]^2+R_{pqr}}\ ,$$

$$\rho=\tfrac{1}{2}(L_{r/pq}-L_{pq/r})+\sqrt{[\tfrac{1}{2}(L_{r/pq}-L_{pq/r})]^2+R_{pqr}}\ .$$

The algebraic simplifications for the above forms have been made in the same way by which equations (4.7) were obtained.

It can readily be seen that the indexes in (4.9) satisfy the time reversal and the factor reversal tests.

Condition (4.8) would imply that the "factor reversal test" is satisfied. In order to see that the "time reversal test" is satisfied, we consider, for example, the equation in π:

$$\pi^2 - \frac{\pi(A'-B'-C')}{V_0} - \frac{V_1}{V_0} = 0.$$

If the subscripts "0" and "1" are interchanged, A', B', C' will change respectively to -A', -B', -C', and V_0 and V_1 respectively to V_1 and V_0. If, in the above equation, we make these changes and change π to $1/\pi^*$, we get the same equation, namely,

$$\pi^{*2} - \pi^* \frac{(A'-B'-C')}{V_0} - \frac{V_1}{V_0} = 0.$$

This shows that the "time reversal test" is satisfied.

4.7 The Formulae for Four or More Factors: The derivation of the indexes may be extended to four or more factors. In case of four factors, the amplitude, α_{pqrs}, taking s as the fourth factor, will consist of eight components of which four will be the four main effects and the other four will be the four three-factor interactions. In case of five factors, the amplitude,

α_{pqrst}, taking t as the fifth factor, will consist of 16 components of which five will be the main effects, ten, the three-factor interactions, and one, the five-factor interaction.

The factorial combinations (1, 1,...,1) and (0, 0,...,0) are involved in the amplitude. The first one corresponds to the combination of all factors at level 1, and the second to the combination of all factors at level 0 (control). All effects and interactions will appear as plus in the combination (1, 1,...,1), whereas in the combination (0, 0,...,0), the effects with an even number of factors will occur as plus, and the effects with an odd number of factors as minus. The amplitude which represents the difference of the two combinations will therefore contain only those effects and/or interactions which have an odd number of factors in them. Hence, whatever may be the number of factors, no component in the amplitude will have an interaction lower than a three-factor interaction. The amplitude will therefore involve, besides the main effects, the three-factor interactions, the five-factor interactions, etc. which can easily be ignored. It is this fact which renders the construction of the indexes possible and reasonable at the same time. In respect of four factors, the equations corresponding to (4.6) will be eight in number of which four will correspond to the four main effects and the other four to the three-factor interactions. Ignoring these three-factor interactions, the equations may be solved in exactly the same way, and the four indexes obtained to represent the four main effects. The right-hand sides of the resulting eight equations would be A", B", C", D", A"B"C", A"B"D", A"C"D", and B"C"D" with similar meanings for A", B", C", D", etc. If equations corresponding to A", -B", -C", -D", A"B"C", A"B"D", A"C"D", -B"C"D" are added, we shall get an equation of the type

$$V_0''(\pi-\kappa\rho\alpha)=A''-B''-C''-D'',$$

where the three-factor interactions are taken as zeros.

Similarly, three other equations may be formed, and the solutions obtained as in the case of three factors.

The procedure of simplification as indicated above for four factors will afford a hint for the simplification in the general case. It will be noted that in the eight equations to be added, the sign of a three-factor interaction is determined by the signs of the main effects in the set. For instance, B"C"D" occurs with a minus sign, because this is the product of -B", -C", and -D" occurring in the same set.

Finally, the indexes corresponding to the four main effects would be obtained as

$$\pi=\frac{1}{2}(L_{p/qrs}-L_{qrs/p})+\sqrt{[\frac{1}{2}(L_{p/qrs}-L_{qrs/p})]^2+R_{pqrs}},$$

$$\kappa=\frac{1}{2}(L_{q/prs}-L_{prs/q})+\sqrt{[\frac{1}{2}(L_{q/prs}-L_{prs/q})]^2+R_{pqrs}},$$

$$\rho=\frac{1}{2}(L_{r/pqs}-L_{pqs/r})+\sqrt{[\frac{1}{2}(L_{r/pqs}-L_{pqs/r})]^2+R_{pqrs}},$$

$$\sigma=\frac{1}{2}(L_{s/pqr}-L_{pqr/s})+\sqrt{[\frac{1}{2}(L_{s/pqr}-L_{pqr/s})]^2+R_{pqrs}},$$

where σ is the index for the fourth factor, s.

The formulae for any number of factors may easily be written down from the symmetry.

It will be noticed that only 10=(2n+2) of the 16 combinations of a 2^n-experiment (n=4) are involved in the above formulae. Utilizing only a single replicate of these ten combinations, the above formulae might be written in abridged notations as

$$\pi=\frac{1}{2}(\frac{p}{(1)}-\frac{qrs}{p})+\sqrt{[\frac{1}{2}(\frac{p}{(1)}-\frac{qrs}{p})]^2+\frac{pqrs}{(1)}}$$

$$\kappa=\frac{1}{2}(\frac{q}{(1)}-\frac{prs}{q})+\sqrt{[\frac{1}{2}(\frac{q}{(1)}-\frac{prs}{q})]^2+\frac{pqrs}{(1)}}$$

(4.10)

$$\rho=\frac{1}{2}(\frac{r}{(1)}-\frac{pqs}{r})+\sqrt{[\frac{1}{2}(\frac{r}{(1)}-\frac{pqs}{r})]^2+\frac{pqrs}{(1)}}$$

$$\sigma=\frac{1}{2}(\frac{s}{(1)}-\frac{pqr}{s})+\sqrt{[\frac{1}{2}(\frac{s}{(1)}-\frac{pqr}{s})]^2+\frac{pqrs}{(1)}},$$

where, as usual, (1) represents the yield corresponding to $p_0q_0r_0s_0$ (control), and p, the yield corresponding to $p_1q_0r_0s_0$, etc., etc.

4.8 <u>What Fractional Replicate the Treatment Combinations Constitute</u>: It has been noticed that only a special sub-set of the factorial combinations enters into the formulae. This sub-set constitutes a special kind of an irregular fractional plan.

It is well known that the total number of factorial combinations, s^n, of n factors at s levels each may be denoted by points of an n-dimensional lattice with n axes as $x_1, x_2, \ldots, x_n$, where each axis will have s points being given by the elements of the Galois field GF(s). In this particular case, s=2, and the elements are 0 and 1.

For the n factors, P, Q, R, S,...,T, let us denote by the notation $PQRS\ldots T_i$ (interaction) that set of the factorial combinations for which $x_1+x_2+\ldots+x_n=i$ (i=0,1). If, for instance, PQRS=1, is used as the identity relationship in the half replicate of a 2^4-experiment, the symbol $PQRS_0$ will be used to denote the set of combinations given by $x_1+x_2+x_3+x_4=0$ (mod. 2). Again, all the four quarter replicates of a 2^4-experiment defined by the identity relationship, PQR=PQS=RS=1 will be given by

(i) $PQR_0=PQS_0=RS_0=1$

(ii) $PQR_0=PQS_1=RS_1=1$

(iii) $PQR_1=PQS_0=RS_1=1$

(iv) $PQR_1=PQS_1=RS_0=1$.

Each of the above four arrangements would give a quarter replicate, and two of them together, a half replicate. The quarter replicates given by (i) and (ii) together would be the same as the half replicate given by PQR=1. In this half replicate, the interaction PQR gets confounded with the mean, and that it is so is borne by the fact that in (i) and (ii) PQR has the common suffix 0.

In the index number formulae for four factors, the ten factorial combinations involved are

(i)	0 0 0 0	1 1 1 1
(ii)	1 0 0 0	0 1 1 1
(iii)	0 1 0 0	1 0 1 1
(iv)	0 0 1 0	1 1 0 1
(v)	0 0 0 1	1 1 1 0 .

The above points in pairs are given by the following relationships:

$$\text{(i)} \quad (PQ)_0=(RS)_0=(PS)_0=(PR)_0=(QS)_0=(QR)_0=(PQRS)_0=1$$

$$\text{(ii)} \quad (PQ)_1=(RS)_0=(PS)_1=(PR)_1=(QS)_0=(QR)_0=(PQRS)_1=1$$

$$\text{(4.11)(iii)} \quad (PQ)_1=(RS)_0=(PS)_0=(PR)_0=(QS)_1=(QR)_1=(PQRS)_1=1$$

$$\text{(iv)} \quad (PQ)_0=(RS)_1=(PS)_0=(PR)_1=(QS)_0=(QR)_1=(PQRS)_1=1$$

$$\text{(v)} \quad (PQ)_0=(RS)_1=(PS)_1=(PR)_0=(QS)_1=(QR)_0=(PQRS)_1=1$$

Equations (4.11) would suggest that the ten combinations of a 2^4-experiment would represent a $\frac{5}{8}$ fractional replicate. Since none of the two-factor or four-factor interactions has the same suffix 0 or 1, none of them will get confounded with the mean.

It will be clear from the distribution of the suffixes that the eighth replicates (ii), (iii), (iv), and (v) of (4.11) constitute a half replicate given by PQRS=1, and (i) gives an additional eighth replicate.

In case of a 2^4-experiment, there are six two-factor interactions and one four-factor interaction making up a total of seven such interactions. All the seven are involved in the above defining contrasts.

In the same manner, all the two-factor and four-factor interactions, 15 in number, will form the defining contrasts for the sixteenth replicates in case of a 2^5-experiment. As the index number formulae for five factors will involve twelve factorial combinations, these twelve combinations will be covered by six of the sixteenth replicates.

Such an irregular fractional plan, that is, a plan of the type of $r/2^n$ experiment (where r is not a power of 2) would ordinarily lead to correlated estimates of the main effects and, as such, the analysis will not be as straightforward as is in a full orthogonalized plan.

From the point of view of easiness in calculation, therefore, the indexes in (4.10) may have a place when a ready indication of the main effects is called for. Such index numbers will have all the advantages of index numbers as in economic fields. On the other hand, these indexes may also be used as multi-dimensional index number formulae in economic fields in situations involving more than 2 factors [22,27].

It is thus noticed that (2n+2) combinations of a 2^n-factorial, which enter into the construction of multi-dimensional index number formulae, constitute a special type of an irregular fractional replicate. How good is such a fractional replicate plan (called the "Index Plan") as a design in agro-biological experiments has been examined in [8].

CHAPTER FIVE

A CONNECTION OF THE FACTORIAL INDEXES WITH THEIL'S B.L.U. INDEXES

5.0 Chapter Summary: Professor Theil [25] gave the derivation of the best linear (B.L.) index number formulae for price and quantity. In an application of the formulae to Dutch import and export data, Kloek and DeWit [16] found that there is some slight, though persistent, bias to the effect that the index vectors yield larger current values than the individual data do. As this feature is related conceptually to the factor reversal test, they considered it desirable to devise a method which would control this bias on the average and worked out what may be called the best linear average unbiased (B.L.A.U.) index number. In this chapter we indicate what relationship the B.L. and the B.L.A.U. indexes bear to the factorial indexes, that is, to those obtained through the factorial approach. We conclude that the factorial indexes appear to compare well with the B.L.A.U. indexes. Incidentally, it is also pointed out in this chapter that it might be possible to obtain a closer algebraic approximation to the B.L. index number formulae than visualized by the proponents of these index number formulae.

5.1 B.L. Index Numbers: Retaining, as far as possible, the notation of the previous authors, (Theil [25], Kloek and DeWit [16]), we may briefly indicate here the derivation of the B.L. and B.L.A.U. index number formulae to the extent needed for the present purpose.

A set of quantities and a set of corresponding prices for N commodities may be represented in the form of two T×N matrices as follows:

$$Q=\begin{bmatrix} q_{11} & \cdots & q_{1N} \\ \cdots & \cdots & \cdots \\ q_{T1} & \cdots & q_{1N} \end{bmatrix}, \quad P=\begin{bmatrix} p_{11} & \cdots & p_{1N} \\ \cdots & \cdots & \cdots \\ p_{T1} & \cdots & p_{TN} \end{bmatrix},$$

where T is the number of periods for which the quantities and the prices are available. The cross-value matrix C is given by C=PQ', where Q' is the transpose of Q. The elements of C are the cross-value aggregates of the quantities of any period priced at the prices of any period. The B.L. price index and quantity index vectors, p and q, are found by minimizing the sum of squares of the elements of the matrix E of cross-value discrepancies, where

$$E = C - pq' \tag{5.1}$$

In other words, p and q are such that

$$tr(EE')=tr(E'E)=\text{minimum}. \tag{5.2}$$

Differentiating (5.2) partially with respect to p and q, equating the derivatives to zero, and suitably rearranging the terms, the necessary conditions are obtained as

$$(CC'-p'p\cdot q'qI)p=0 \tag{5.3}$$

$$(C'C-p'p\cdot q'qI)q=0 \tag{5.4}$$

From (5.3) and (5.4) it will be clear that p and q are the characteristic vectors of CC' and C'C respectively, and that CC' and C'C have the same set of characteristic roots,

$$p'p\cdot q'q=\lambda^2=\lambda(\text{say})$$

In order to satisfy (5.2), the characteristic vectors corresponding to the largest root are taken. (See Kloek and DeWit [16])

5.2 Indexes for a Two-Year Period: To derive the indexes for a two-year period (i.e., when T=2), the cross-value matrix is taken in the form

$$C=\begin{bmatrix} 1 & L_q \\ L_p & L_pL_q(1+\eta) \end{bmatrix}$$

where $\Sigma_{i=1}^{N}p_{1i}q_{1i}$ has been taken as unity, and L_p and L_q are Laspeyres' price and quantity indexes.[5] η is defined as

$$P_p=L_p(1+\eta), \tag{5.5}$$

[5]The previous authors have used P and Q to denote Laspeyres' price and quantity indexes. In this paper, L_p and L_q have been substituted for P and Q.

where P_p is Paasche's price index. η is small. From equations (5.3) and (5.4), the price and quantity indexes[6] are derived as

$$\text{(5.6)} \qquad \pi \simeq L_p[1+\eta \frac{L_q^2}{1+L_q^2}]; \quad \kappa \simeq L_q[1+\eta \frac{L_p^2}{1+L_p^2}].$$

In the above derivation, higher powers of η have been neglected. If it is assumed that $p'p=q'q=\lambda$, the matrix of cross-value discrepancies reduces to

$$E_0 \simeq \eta \frac{L_pL_q}{D} \begin{bmatrix} L_pL_q & -L_p \\ -L_q & 1 \end{bmatrix},$$

and the sum of squares of all the four cross-value discrepancies comes out as

$$\text{(5.7)} \qquad tr(E_0E_0') \simeq \eta^2 \frac{L_p^2L_q^2}{D},$$

where $D=(1+L_p^2)(1+L_q^2)$.

5.3 <u>B.L.A.U. Index Numbers</u>: In order to minimize the effect of bias arising out of the formulae not satisfying the factor reversal test, Kloek and DeWit minimize the sum of squares of the elements of E subject to the constraint,

$$\text{(5.8)} \qquad trE=trC-p'q=0.$$

If the diagonal elements of the matrix E were separately restrained to be zero, the index number formulae would have satisfied the factor reversal test. But this is not done. In preference to this, Kloek and DeWit use the restraint (5.8), as this restraint would remove the bias on the average. After elaborate simplifications, the price and quantity indexes, $P_{\hat{\mu}}$ and $Q_{\hat{\mu}}$, are obtained as

$$P_{\hat{\mu}} \simeq L_p\{1+\eta L_q \frac{L_q(1+L_p^2)-(L_p-L_q)}{D+(L_p-L_q)^2}\},$$

---

[6]The previous authors used P_0 and Q_0 for the price and quantity indexes.

$$Q_{\hat{\mu}} \simeq L_q \{1+\eta L_p \frac{L_p(1+L_q^2)+(L_p-L_q)}{D+(L_p-L_q)^2}\} .$$

The sum of squares of the elements of the corresponding E matrix, $E_{\hat{\mu}}$, is shown to reduce to

$$tr(E_{\hat{\mu}}E'_{\hat{\mu}}) \simeq 2\eta^2 \frac{L_p^2 L_q^2}{D+(L_p-L_q)^2} .$$

The above results are quoted from Kloek and DeWit [16].

A comparison of (5.9) with (5.7) would reveal that use of constraint (5.8) to cover the bias leads nearly to doubling the sum of squares of the cross-value discrepancies.

5.4 Feasibility of Closer Algebraic Approximation to B.L. Index Numbers: Denoting the two periods as 0 and 1, the cross-value matrix C may be written as

$$C = \begin{bmatrix} a & aL_q \\ aL_p & aL_pL_q(1+\eta) \end{bmatrix} ,$$

where $a=\Sigma p_0 q_0$, $b=\Sigma p_0 q_1$, $c=\Sigma p_1 q_0$, and $d=\Sigma p_1 q_1$. $\eta=(ad-bc)/bc$. The characteristic roots are given by the equation

$$(\underline{\lambda})^2-\underline{\lambda}a^2(1+L_q^2+L_p^2+L_p^2L_q^2+2L_p^2L_q^2\eta+L_p^2L_q^2\eta^2)+a^4L_p^2L_q^2\eta^2=0.$$

In the derivation of the price and quantity indexes as in [25,16], the terms ignored appear to be

(i) $$a^4L_p^2L_q^2\eta^2=(ad-bc)^2$$
and
(ii) $$-\underline{\lambda}a^2L_p^2L_q^2\eta^2=-\underline{\lambda}(ad-bc)^2/a^2.$$

If only (i) is ignored, and (ii) retained, the price and quantity indexes would, following the same steps, reduce to

$$\pi \simeq \frac{L_p+L_q(V_1/V_0)}{1+L_q^2} ,$$

$$\kappa \simeq \frac{L_q+L_p(V_1/V_0)}{1+L_p^2} ,$$

where $V_1/V_0=\Sigma p_1 q_1/\Sigma p_0 q_0$.

For this order of approximation, that is, when $(ad-bc)^2$ is taken as zero, the indexes satisfy the "time reversal" test. (Incidentally, it may be observed here that Theil's B.L. indexes also satisfy the "time reversal" test; this may easily be shown to be the case when no approximation is made in deriving the indexes).

A closer algebraic approximation to the indexes may perhaps be obtained when higher powers of $4(ad-bc)^2/(a^2+b^2+c^2+d^2)$ only are ignored. In that case, the price and the quantity indexes would reduce to

$$\pi \simeq \frac{\{L_p+L_q(V_1/V_0)\}\{1+L_p^2+L_q^2+(V_1/V_0)^2\}}{(1+L_q^2)^2+\{L_p+L_q(V_1/V_0)\}^2}$$

and

$$\kappa \simeq \frac{\{L_q+L_p(V_1/V_0)\}\{1+L_p^2+L_q^2+(V_1/V_0)^2\}}{(1+L_p^2)^2+\{L_q+L_p(V_1/V_0)\}^2} .$$

5.5 <u>B.L.A.U. Index Numbers and Index Numbers Obtained Through the Factorial Approach</u>: It would have been ideal if the indexes could have been found so that, separately, $a=P_0Q_0$, $b=P_0Q_1$, $c=P_1Q_0$, and $d=P_1Q_1$, where P_0, P_1, and Q_0, Q_1 represent the price and the quantity vectors, p and q, respectively. In that event, the indexes would have satisfied the factor reversal test, besides reducing the sum of squares of elements of the E matrix to zero. But this goal was not reached. In order to make the indexes satisfy the factor reversal test on an average, Kloek and DeWit [16] minimize the sum of squares of elements of the E matrix subject to the restraint,

$$(a-P_0Q_0)+(d-P_1Q_1)=0. \tag{5.10}$$

It will now be shown that the price index, P_1/P_0, and the quantity index, Q_1/Q_0, as obtained previously [4,24] through the factorial approach compare well with B.L.A.U. indexes.

Let A be an orthogonal matrix given as

$$A=\frac{1}{\sqrt{2}}\begin{bmatrix}+1 & +1\\ -1 & +1\end{bmatrix}.$$

Also let, $p^*=AP$, $q^*=Aq$, and $C^*=ACA'$, where A' is the transpose of A, and p and q are the price and quantity vectors. C is transformed to C^*; p and q, respectively, to p^* and q^*. The coordinates of the price vectors, P_0, P_1, and those of the quantity vector, Q_0, Q_1, are respectively changed to P_0^*, P_1^* and Q_0^*, Q_1^*. Under this transformation, the characteristic roots of CC' and $C'C$ will be the same as those of $C^*C^{*\prime}$ and $C^{*\prime}C^*$ respectively. Therefore, in place of the cross-value matrix C, we may use the matrix

$$C^*=\begin{bmatrix}M & \underline{Q}\\ \underline{P} & (\underline{PQ})\end{bmatrix},$$

where $M=\frac{1}{2}(a+b+c+d)$,[7] $\underline{Q}=\frac{1}{2}(-a+b-c+d)$, $\underline{P}=\frac{1}{2}(-a-b+c+d)$, and $\underline{PQ}=\frac{1}{2}(a-b-c+d)$.

If the elements of the corresponding E^* matrix are each equated to zero, we get the following equations.

(i) $$\frac{+P_0Q_0+P_1Q_0+P_0Q_1+P_1Q_1}{2}=M,$$

(ii) $$\frac{-P_0Q_0+P_1Q_0-P_0Q_1+P_1Q_1}{2}=\underline{P},$$

(iii) $$\frac{-P_0Q_0-P_1Q_0+P_0Q_1+P_1Q_1}{2}=\underline{Q},$$

(iv) $$\frac{+P_0Q_0-P_1Q_0-P_0Q_1+P_1Q_1}{2}=(\underline{PQ}).$$

The above equations would lead to

(v) $$\frac{V_0(\pi+1)(\kappa+1)}{2}=M,$$

(vi) $$\frac{V_0(\pi-1)(\kappa+1)}{2}=\underline{P},$$

(vii) $$\frac{V_0(\pi+1)(\kappa-1)}{2}=\underline{Q},$$

---

[7]In factorial analysis, M is usually written for (a+b+c+d)/4.

(viii) $$\frac{V_0(\pi-1)(\kappa-1)}{2} = (\underline{PQ}).$$

where $P_1/P_0=\pi$ (required price index) and $Q_1/Q_0=\kappa$ (required quantity index). If equations (vi) and (vii) are solved for π and κ, the price and the quantity indexes as given by Stuvel [24] would be obtained (see also Chapter Three) as

$$\pi=\frac{L_p-L_q}{2} + \sqrt{(\frac{L_p-L_q}{2})^2 + V_1/V_0} ,$$

$$\kappa=\frac{L_q-L_p}{2} + \sqrt{(\frac{L_q-L_p}{2})^2 + V_1/V_0} .$$

If the values of π and κ as obtained above are substituted in the elements of the E* matrix, two of its elements would be separately zero, and, at the same time, the sum of the diagonal elements will automatically be reduced to zero. Moreover, the indexes will satisfy the factor reversal test.

Ignoring terms like $(ad-bc)^2/(b+c)^3$ and smaller terms, the sum of squares of elements of the E* matrix may be reduced to

(5.11) $$2\frac{(ad-bc)^2}{(b+c)^2} .$$

(5.11) may be compared with (5.9) or with twice the value of (5.7) which is

(5.12) $$\frac{2a^2(ad-bc)^2}{(a^2+c^2)(a^2+b^2)} .$$

As it is, (5.11) may be slightly larger than (5.12). A comparison of the two sums of squares will be valid only where the order of approximation in the two procedures is comparable.

It will be seen, therefore, that the factorial indexes compare favorably with B.L.A.U. indexes in view of the fact that the factorial indexes satisfy the factor reversal and the time reversal tests and that these indexes are sufficiently simple and are easily amenable to extension to any number of factors.

CHAPTER SIX

A GENERALIZATION OF STUVEL'S AVERAGING PROCEDURE

6.0 Chapter Summary: Stuvel's [24] new indexes depend upon taking an average of two identities. The averaging procedure is generalized in this chapter providing additional index number formulae. Stuvel's notations are retained.

6.1 Stuvel's Procedure: Taking 0 as the base period and n as the current period, the quantity relative and the price relative for the ith commodity, as defined by Stuvel, are $q_n^i=Q_n^i/Q_0^i$ and $p_n^i=P_n^i/P_0^i$, respectively. The value of the commodity exchanged in the base period is $V_0^i=P_0^iQ_0^i$ and in the current period is $V_n^i=P_n^iQ_n^i$. Summing up for all commodities,

$$V_0\equiv\sum_i V_0^i \text{ and } V_n\equiv\sum_i V_n^i\ .$$

In deriving the formulae, Stuvel utilizes the arithmetic mean of the identities,

$$(6.1)\qquad V_n^i-V_0^i=V_0^i(p_n^iq_n^i-1)=V_0^i\{p_n^i(q_n^i-1)+(p_n^i-1)\},$$

$$(6.2)\qquad V_n^i-V_0^i=V_0^i(p_n^iq_n^i-1)=V_0^i\{q_n^i(p_n^i-1)+(q_n^i-1)\}$$

in the form

$$(6.3)\quad V_n^i-V_0^i=V_0^i(p_n^iq_n^i-1)=V_0^i\{\frac{p_n^i+1}{2}\ (q_n^i-1)+\frac{q_n^i+1}{2}\ (p_n^i-1)\}.$$

Equation (6.3) provides an expression for the change in value in which the changes in quantity and in price appear as additive components. This expression is then summed over all commodities and the components are made to satisfy the relationships:

$$(6.4)\qquad A=V_0\frac{p_n+1}{2}\ (q_n-1)=\sum_i V_0^i\frac{p_n^i+1}{2}\ (q_n^i-1),$$

$$(6.5)\qquad B=V_0\frac{q_n+1}{2}\ (p_n-1)=\sum_i V_0^i\frac{q_n^i+1}{2}\ (p_n^i-1),$$

where $A+B=V_n-V_0$, and q_n and p_n are the required indexes for quantity and price. The solution of (6.4) and (6.5) leads to the formulae for q_n and p_n.

6.2 <u>A Generalization</u>: Instead of taking the arithmetic mean of identities (6.1) and (6.2) as Stuvel did, (6.1) and (6.2) could have been averaged with weights $\{1+a(p,q)\}/2$ and $\{1+a(q,p)\}/2$ respectively, where $a(p,q)$ denotes an alternating function of p,q, i.e., a function changing sign upon the interchange of p and q. The weighted average will take the following form:

$$(6.6)\qquad V_0(pq-1)=\tfrac{1}{2}V_0\{(p+1)+a(p,q)(p-1)\}(q-1)+\tfrac{1}{2}V_0\{(q+1)+a(q,p)(q-1)\}(p-1).$$

The above reduces to the arithmetic mean of (6.1) and (6.2) when $a(p,q)=0$.

According to Stuvel, the p, q are determined by the equations:

$$(6.7)\qquad \tfrac{1}{2}V_0\{p+1+a(p,q)(p-1)\}(q-1)=\tfrac{1}{2}\,\Sigma\, V_0^i\{p^i+1+a(p^i,q^i)(p^i-1)\}(q^i-1)=\bar{A}$$

and

$$(6.8)\qquad \tfrac{1}{2}V_0\{q+1+a(q,p)(q-1)\}(p-1)=\tfrac{1}{2}\,\Sigma\, V_0^i\{q^i+1+a(q^i,p^i)(q^i-1)\}(p^i-1)=\bar{B}.$$

The subscript n is dropped from p and q for the sake of simplicity of notation and will be omitted henceforth.

The addition of (6.7) and (6.8) gives $V_0(pq-1)= V_n-V_0=\bar{A}+\bar{B}$. Hence,

$$(6.9)\qquad pq=V_n/V_0.$$

The subtraction of (6.8) from (6.7) gives

$$V_0(q-p)+V_0a(p,q)(p-1)(q-1)=\bar{A}-\bar{B},$$

or

$$(6.10)\quad V_0\{1-a(p,q)\}q-V_0\{1+a(p,q)\}p+(V_n+V_0)a(p,q)=\bar{A}-\bar{B}.$$

Different formulae for p and q (i.e., formulae for the

indexes of price and quantity) may be obtained for different functions a(p,q). In particular,

(i) a(p,q)=1 gives Laspeyres' price index and Paasche's quantity index.

(ii) a(p,q)=-1 gives Paasche's price index and Laspeyres' quantity index.

(iii) $a(p,q)=\dfrac{\Sigma V_0^i q^i - \Sigma V_0^i p^i}{\Sigma V_0^i q^i + \Sigma V_0^i p^i}$ gives Fisher's price and quantity indexes.

(iv) $a(p,q)=\dfrac{p^t - q^t}{p^t + q^t}$ gives, for t=-1,

$p=\sqrt{\dfrac{V_n}{V_0}\left(\dfrac{B+V_0}{A+V_0}\right)}$ and $q=\sqrt{\dfrac{V_n}{V_0}\left(\dfrac{A+V_0}{B+V_0}\right)}$, and so on, where A and B are the corresponding quantity and price components.

Situations (i) and (ii) would give what would have been obtained if the equations were constructed separately from identity (6.1) or (6.2).

We may retain only those formulae which satisfy the "factor reversal" and "time-reversal" tests. It is, however, seen that, whatever might be the form of the function a(p,q), the factor-reversal test will be satisfied by virtue of (6.9) and (6.10). But, the situation is different with regard to the time-reversal test. In order that it be satisfied, the function a(p,q) must be of a special class. One class appears to be that of functions a(p,q) which reduce to a(q,p) when reciprocals of p and q are substituted for p and q in a(p,q). This is satisfied, for instance, by form (iv), or by forms expressed as a sum of such terms, where t=1,2,3,....

The form indicated by (iii) is also of this class.

If the time subscripts are interchanged, V_n changes to V_0 and V_0 to V_n, and the equation corresponding to euqation (6.10) is obtained in the following form:

$$(6.11)\quad V_n\{1-a(p',q')\}q'-V_n\{1+a(p',q')\}p'+(V_n+V_0)a(p',q')=\bar{A}'-\bar{B}'.$$

where p' and q' are the reciprocals of p and q, and $\bar{A}'$ and $\bar{B}'$ are given by

$$(6.12)\quad \tfrac{1}{2}V_n\{p'+1+a(p',q')(p'-1)\}(q'-1) =\tfrac{1}{2}\Sigma V_n^i\{p^{i'}+1+a(p^{i'},q^{i'})(p^{i'}-1)\}(q^{i'}-1)=\bar{A}'$$

and

$$(6.13)\quad \tfrac{1}{2}V_n\{q'+1+a(q',p')(q'-1)\}(p'-1) =\tfrac{1}{2}\Sigma V_n^i\{q^{i'}+1+a(q^{i'},p^{i'})(q^{i'}-1)\}(p^{i'}-1)=\bar{B}'.$$

It can easily be verified that if the form of the function a(p,q) is of the special class considered here, $\bar{A}'$ reduces to $-\bar{A}$ and $\bar{B}'$ to $-\bar{B}$.

In order that the time reversal test be satisfied, the values of p' and q' in (6.11) should be the reciprocals of the values of p and q in (6.10). In other words, this means that the equation derived from (6.11) by the substitution of 1/p, 1/q, $-\bar{A}$, and $-\bar{B}$ for p', q', $\bar{A}'$, and $\bar{B}'$, respectively, should be identically the same as (6.10). This requirement is satisfied. (A similar reasoning was used in section 6 of Chapter Four).

CHAPTER SEVEN

INDEX NUMBERS OF PRICES AND QUANTITIES FOR AN ARBITRARY NUMBER OF PERIODS THROUGH THE FACTORIAL APPROACH

7.0 Chapter Summary: This chapter provides index number formulae for price and quantity for an arbitrary number of periods (or geographical units), based on the "factorial approach." The formulae are obtained by solving a system of nonlinear simultaneous equations. Two simple numerical examples with opposite economic trends are eventually presented illustrating the calculations.

7.1 Introduction: As indicated in Chapter Five, Theil [25] provided what he called the Best Linear index numbers of prices and quantities for an arbitrary number of periods (or geographical units) which satisfy the requirement that the total sum of squares of the discrepancies between true and index constructed cross-values is minimized. The analysis is mathematically related in some sense to "principal component" analysis. The price and quantity indices are obtained from the solution of the characteristic vectors.

Also, Geary [15C] and Khamis [15D] proposed a new class of index numbers for multilateral price and quantity comparisons. These are based on the concepts of "exchange rate" of the currency and "average price" of a commodity. Prasad Rao [19A] studied problems, in the related contexts, concerning the existence and uniqueness of this new class of index numbers. The index numbers are obtained from the solution of a system of linear equations.

While both the above approaches, which are mathematically elegant, can be exploited to provide index numbers for price and quantity, one still wishes if it were possible to get easily computable index number formulae for the purpose, - formulae that would be relatively easy to handle, yet having a justified statistical meaning.

In this chapter, we present an approach, based on a generalization of Stuvel's "new indexes" [24], which would provide price and quantity comparisons for a number of periods (or geographical units) in the form of *concrete* formulae. The formulae are based on the solution of a system of nonlinear simultaneous equations. It is indicated, *inter alias*, that the factorial approach is related, in some sense, to Theil's approach in the set-up of Least Squares solutions.

In the last section, we present the indices for price and quantity in the situation when prices and quantities are considered separately. These separate indices reveal in a way an implication of the factorial approach.

7.2 Stuvel's Equations Rewritten: It is observed that the right hand sides of the equations (3.5.2) and (3.5.3) (see Chapter Three) can be derived from the left hand sides, if, according to the Divisia indexes, the identities, $\Sigma p_0q_0=P_0Q_0$, $\Sigma p_1q_0=P_1Q_0$, $\Sigma p_0q_1=P_0Q_1$ and $\Sigma p_1q_1=P_1Q_1$, are inserted, writing $\pi=P_1/P_0$ and $\kappa=Q_1/Q_0$. (In Chapter Three a * was put on P_0Q_0, P_1Q_0, P_0Q_1 and P_1Q_1. This is avoided here to simplify notations.)

Equations (3.5.2) and (3.5.3) are only two of the four possible equations which can be written as follows:

$$\begin{bmatrix} 4\mu \\ 2\mathcal{P} \\ 2\mathcal{Q} \\ 2(\mathcal{PQ}) \end{bmatrix} = \begin{bmatrix} +1 & +1 & +1 & +1 \\ -1 & +1 & -1 & +1 \\ -1 & -1 & +1 & +1 \\ +1 & -1 & -1 & +1 \end{bmatrix} \begin{bmatrix} \Sigma p_0q_0 \\ \Sigma p_1q_0 \\ \Sigma p_0q_1 \\ \Sigma p_1q_1 \end{bmatrix}$$

$$= \begin{bmatrix} +1 & +1 & +1 & +1 \\ -1 & +1 & -1 & +1 \\ -1 & -1 & +1 & +1 \\ +1 & -1 & -1 & +1 \end{bmatrix} \begin{bmatrix} V_{00}(1) \\ V_{00}(\pi) \\ V_{00}(\kappa) \\ V_{00}(\pi\kappa) \end{bmatrix} .$$

In the column vector of the last expression, we substitute in terms of the Divisia indexes, and this expression will represent the left hand side of the equations. In the above, $V_{00}=\Sigma p_0q_0$, and $\mathcal{P}$, $\mathcal{Q}$, $(\mathcal{PQ})$ represent respectively the price effect, the quantity effect and the interaction between price and quantity.

Equations (3.5.2) and (3.5.3) are only two of the four possible equations in the variables π, κ, which come from the four mutually orthogonal linear functions of the four value aggregates, Σp_iq_j, $i,j=0,1$. Any two of these four equations could be utilized to find π and κ. The reasons that we choose (3.5.2) and (3.5.3), the equations giving the price effect and the quantity effect, are explained in Chapter Three (see also Chapter Eight). We also notice that the 4×4 orthogonal matrix shown above is obtained as the direct product,

$$\begin{bmatrix} +1 & +1 \\ -1 & +1 \end{bmatrix} \otimes \begin{bmatrix} +1 & +1 \\ -1 & +1 \end{bmatrix},$$

and that the column vector in (π,κ), omitting V_{00} is correspondingly written as the left direct product.

$$\begin{bmatrix}1\\ \pi\end{bmatrix} \otimes \begin{bmatrix}1\\ \kappa\end{bmatrix}.$$

<u>7.3 Statistical Preliminaries</u>: If, in regression analysis, we are given n pairs of data points, (y_i,x_i), $i=0,1,\ldots,(n-1)$, pertaining to the n levels of a factor, where y_i is either a single response observation, or a total of, or an average over r replications of responses, corresponding to the level i of x, we can have an exact fit of the polynomial equation of the (n-1)th degree, $y=a_0+a_1x+a_2x^2+\ldots+a_{n-1}x^{n-1}$. By a suitable transformation made on the x-values, we can write this polynomial equation in an equivalent form, $y=b_0+b_1X_1+b_2X_2+\ldots+b_{n-1}X_{n-1}$, where X_i, $i=0,1,2,\ldots,n-1$, represents the ith degree polynomial in x, such that the b_i's are obtained as mutually orthogonal (linear) functions of the y's. The polynomials X_i are referred to as orthogonal polynomials. The coefficient b_i represents the contribution of the ith degree effect to the response. When the points x_i are equally spaced, such as having the values $0,1,2,\ldots,n-1$, the values of such orthogonal polynomials are easily calculated corresponding to the x-values, (that is, the levels of x), and are found extensively tabulated for ready reference in any Statistical Tables for almost any value of n. For the theoretical basis of such calculations, the interested reader may refer to DeLury [10A]. The values of such orthogonal polynomials at the points $x=0,1,2,\ldots,n-1$ are always provided as integers, which is made possible by multiplying the polynomial values by a scaling factor. We provide these values for n=2, n=3, and n=4.

n=2

	(0)	(1)
X_0:	+1	+1
X_1:	-1	+1

n=3

	(0)	(1)	(2)
X_0:	+1	+1	+1
X_1:	-1	0	+1
X_2:	1	-2	+1

n=4

	(0)	(1)	(2)	(3)
X_0:	1	+1	+1	+1
X_1:	-3	-1	+1	+3
X_2:	+1	-1	-1	+1
X_3:	-1	+3	-3	+1

In general, the matrix of the values of these orthogonal polynomials may be written as

$$\underline{O}_n = \begin{bmatrix} 1, & 1, \ldots & 1 \\ \cdots & \cdots & \cdots \\ \underline{\ell}_{n-1} & (\underline{D}_{n-1}) & \end{bmatrix},$$

where $\underline{D}_{n-1}$ is an $(n-1)\times(n-1)$ matrix, and $\underline{\ell}_{n-1}$ is the $(n-1)\times 1$ column vector of the values of the first column of $\underline{O}_n$, except for the first element. We may drop the suffix from $\underline{D}_{n-1}$ and $\underline{\ell}_{n-1}$, as the dimensions will be clear from the context. The matrix $\underline{O}_n$ is such that

$$\underline{O}\,\underline{O}' = \text{Diag}\left[S_0, S_1, S_2, \ldots, S_{n-1}\right],$$

is a diagonal matrix where S_i, $i=0,1,2,\ldots,n-1$, is the sum of squares of the elements of the ith row of $\underline{O}$. Hence, $\underline{O}^{-1}=\underline{O}'$ Diag $\left[\frac{1}{S_0}, \frac{1}{S_1}, \frac{1}{S_2}, \ldots, \frac{1}{S_{n-1}}\right]$. It can be easily verified that

(i) $\underline{D}^{-1}\underline{\ell}=-\underline{1}$

(ii) $\underline{1}'\underline{D}^{-1}\underline{\ell}=-(n-1)$,

where $\underline{1}$ is the column vector of 1's.

In the final analysis, that is, in the presentation of the index number formulae in concrete shape, *we only need to know that an orthogonal matrix* $\underline{O}$ *exists with the above mentioned properties.*

7.4 Enunciation of the Problem: In the context of finding the index numbers of price and quantity for the periods, 1,2,...,(n-1), compared to the period 0, we need to find the price vector $\underline{p}=[P_0, P_1, P_2, \ldots, P_{n-1}]'$ and the quantity vector $\underline{q}=[Q_0, Q_1, Q_2, \ldots, Q_{n-1}]'$. Basically, we need (n-1) price indices, $\pi_{0i}=P_i/P_0$, and (n-1) quantity indices, $\kappa_{0i}=Q_i/Q_0$, $i=1,2,\ldots,(n-1)$. Further, the price index π_{0s} is obtained as a chain index given as $\pi_{0s}=\pi_{01}\pi_{12}\cdots\pi_{s-1,s}$, where $\pi_{j,\ell}$ indicates the price index for the period ℓ compared to the period j. Similarly, the quantity index is obtained as a chain index given as $\kappa_{0s}=\kappa_{01}\kappa_{12}\cdots\kappa_{s-1,s}$, with similar interpretation for the quantity index $\kappa_{j,\ell}$. For convenience in notations, we shall denote the vector of price indices as

$$\underline{X} = [x_1, x_1x_2, \ldots, x_1x_2\ldots x_{n-1}]'$$

and the vector of quantity indices as

$$\underline{Y} = [y_1, y_1y_2, \ldots, y_1y_2\ldots y_{n-1}]',$$

where $x_1x_2\ldots x_s=\pi_{0s}$ and $y_1y_2\ldots y_s=\kappa_{0s}$. In the above set-up, we retain the chain indices in the multiplicative form.

Now we visualize in terms of an n^2-factorial experiment involving 2 factors, price and quantity, at n levels each, the levels being 0,1,...,n-1. The n^2 data points are given by the elements of the matrix $\underline{V}=(V_{ij})$, $V_{ij}=\Sigma p_i q_j$, $i,j=0,1,\ldots,n-1$, where the summation sign extends over r commodities. (Incidentally, Theil [25] wrote N for r). Written in full, the value matrix is given as

$$\underline{V} = \begin{bmatrix} V_{00} & V_{01} & V_{0,n-1} \\ V_{10} & V_{11} & V_{1,n-1} \\ \cdots & \cdots & \cdots \\ V_{n-1,0} & V_{n-1,1} \cdots & V_{n-1,n-1} \end{bmatrix} = \underline{P}\ \underline{Q}',$$

where the price matrix $\underline{P}$ and the quantity matrix $\underline{Q}$ are written as

$$\underline{P} = \begin{bmatrix} p_{01} \cdots, p_{0,r} \\ \cdots\cdots \\ \cdots\cdots \\ p_{n-1,1} \cdots p_{n-1,r} \end{bmatrix}, \qquad \underline{Q} = \begin{bmatrix} q_{01} \cdots, q_{0,r} \\ \cdots\cdots \\ \cdots\cdots \\ q_{n-1,1} \cdots q_{n-1,r} \end{bmatrix}.$$

It may be noted here that we shall eventually express the results in terms of the elements of the matrix $(V_{00})^{-1}\underline{V}$, where $V_{00}=\Sigma p_0q_0$.

The n^2 elements of the matrix V will give rise to n^2 mutually orthogonal linear equations representing the effect of the mean (general effect), the ith degree effect of price, the ith degree effect of quantity, and the (i,j)th interaction between the ith degree effect of price and the jth degree effect of quantity, i,j=1,2,...,n-1. In all, therefore, we shall have $1+2(n-1)+(n-1)^2=n^2$ equations. Of these n^2 mutually orthogonal linear equations, we shall need 2(n-1) of them to provide the (n-1) price indices and the (n-1) quantity indices. These 2(n-1) equations will represent the 1st degree, 2nd degree, ...,(n-1)th degree effect of price, and the 1st degree, 2nd degree, ...,(n-1)th degree effect of quantity.

7.5 Solution of the Price Vector and the Quantity Vector: To fix ideas, we write below the 9 equations for a 3^2-factorial experiment, that is, for the number of periods n=3. Price will have two effects, the first degree effect and the second degree effect. Similarly, quantity will have two effects, the first degree effect and the second degree effect.

$$(7.1)\quad \begin{bmatrix} M \\ P_1 \\ P_2 \\ Q_1 \\ (PQ)_{11} \\ (PQ)_{21} \\ Q_2 \\ (PQ)_{12} \\ (PQ)_{22} \end{bmatrix} = \begin{bmatrix} +1 & +1 & +1 & +1 & +1 & +1 & +1 & +1 & +1 \\ -1 & 0 & +1 & -1 & 0 & +1 & -1 & 0 & +1 \\ +1 & -2 & +1 & +1 & -2 & +1 & +1 & -2 & +1 \\ -1 & -1 & -1 & 0 & 0 & 0 & +1 & +1 & +1 \\ +1 & 0 & -1 & 0 & 0 & 0 & -1 & 0 & +1 \\ -1 & +2 & -1 & 0 & 0 & 0 & +1 & -2 & +1 \\ +1 & +1 & +1 & -2 & -2 & -2 & +1 & +1 & +1 \\ -1 & 0 & +1 & 2 & 0 & -2 & -1 & 0 & +1 \\ +1 & -2 & +1 & -2 & +4 & -2 & +1 & -2 & +1 \end{bmatrix} \begin{bmatrix} d(\Sigma p_0q_0/d) \\ d(\Sigma p_1q_0/d) \\ d(\Sigma p_2q_0/d) \\ d(\Sigma p_0q_1/d) \\ d(\Sigma p_1q_1/d) \\ d(\Sigma p_2q_1/d) \\ d(\Sigma p_0q_2/d) \\ d(\Sigma p_1q_2/d) \\ d(\Sigma p_2q_2/d) \end{bmatrix},$$

where $d=\Sigma p_0q_0$. The suffix 1 or 2 associated with P or Q represents respectively the linear and quadratic effect of price and quantity, and the suffix (ij), i,j=1,2, associated with (PQ) represents the interaction between the ith degree effect of price and the jth degree effect of quantity.

It is important to note that a price effect becomes the corresponding quantity effect, and vice versa, if the suffixes i,j of Σp_iq_j are interchanged.

The above 9 equations represent 9 mutually orthogonal linear functions. All except the first are referred to as "comparisons" in the language of Design of Experiments. Usually, a separate dividing factor is associated with each of these comparisons for mutual comparability. The dividing factor will not make any difference in our study, as it will cancel out from both sides of the resulting equations.

The order in which Σp_iq_j is written in the above is relevant.

The above 9×9 matrix is easily recognized as $\underline{O}_3 \otimes \underline{O}_3$. The right hand side of the required equations will be written as

$$\left[\underline{O}_3 \otimes \underline{O}_3\right]\left[\underline{J}\right],$$

where $\underline{J}$ is the outermost column vector of (7.1) and the left hand side as

$$\left[\underline{O}_3 \otimes \underline{O}_3\right]\left[\underline{I}\right],$$

where $\underline{I}$ is given by

$$V_{00}\left[\begin{pmatrix}1\\ \underline{X}\end{pmatrix} \odot \begin{pmatrix}1\\ \underline{Y}\end{pmatrix}\right].$$

It may be recalled that we find $\underline{I}$ from $\underline{J}$ by writing P_iQ_j for Σp_iq_j, according to the Divisia indexes. We then divide both sides by $V_{00}=\Sigma p_0q_0=P_0Q_0$.

Any four of the 9 resulting equations may be utilized to solve for the two price indices x_1, x_1x_2, and the two quantity indices y_1, y_1y_2. We shall adopt for our purpose the 4 equations pertaining to P_1, P_2, and Q_1, Q_2, representing the linear and quadratic effects of price and quantity.

We shall utilize, in general, 2(n-1) of the n^2 equations representing the main degree effects of price and quantity.

Spelled out in full, the four equations will be obtained as

$$\begin{bmatrix}(-1+x_1x_2)(1+y_1+y_1y_2)\\(1-2x_1+x_1x_2)(1+y_1+y_1y_2)\end{bmatrix}=\begin{bmatrix}P_1\\P_2\end{bmatrix}=\begin{bmatrix}\underline{P}\end{bmatrix}$$

$$\begin{bmatrix}(-1+y_1y_2)(1+x_1+x_1x_2)\\(1-2y_1+y_1y_2)(1+x_1+x_1x_2)\end{bmatrix}=\begin{bmatrix}Q_1\\Q_2\end{bmatrix}=\begin{bmatrix}\underline{Q}\end{bmatrix},$$

where $\underline{P}=[P_1,P_2]'$ and $\underline{Q}=[Q_1,Q_2]'$.

At first sight, solution of the above nonlinear simultaneous equations may appear to be intractable. But, the symmetry helps us. We may rearrange the above equations respectively in the following forms:

$$\begin{bmatrix}-1 & 0 & 1\\1 & -2 & 1\end{bmatrix}\begin{bmatrix}1\\x_1\\x_1x_2\end{bmatrix}=\eta^{-1}\underline{P},\ \eta=1+y_1+y_1y_2$$

$$\begin{bmatrix}-1 & 0 & 1\\1 & -2 & 1\end{bmatrix}\begin{bmatrix}1\\y_1\\y_1y_2\end{bmatrix}=\xi^{-1}\underline{Q},\ \xi=1+x_1+x_1x_2,$$

or,

$$\begin{bmatrix}\underline{\ell}\vdots\underline{D}\end{bmatrix}\begin{bmatrix}1\\\underline{X}\end{bmatrix}=\eta^{-1}\underline{P},\quad \begin{bmatrix}\underline{\ell}\vdots\underline{D}\end{bmatrix}\begin{bmatrix}1\\\underline{Y}\end{bmatrix}=\xi^{-1}\underline{Q}$$

That is,

$$[\underline{X}]=\eta^{-1}\underline{D}^{-1}\underline{P}-\underline{D}^{-1}\underline{\ell},$$

$$[\underline{Y}]=\xi^{-1}\underline{D}^{-1}\underline{Q}-\underline{D}^{-1}\underline{\ell}.$$

From the above, we have

(7.2) $$\xi=1+\underline{1}'\underline{X}=1+\underline{1}'[\eta^{-1}\underline{D}^{-1}\underline{P}-\underline{D}^{-1}\underline{\ell}]$$

(7.3) $$\eta=1+1'\underline{Y}=1+\underline{1}'[\xi^{-1}\underline{D}^{-1}\underline{Q}-\underline{D}^{-1}\underline{\ell}],$$

where $\underline{1}$ is the column vector of 1's.

Substituting the value of ξ from (7.2) in (7.3), and after some simplification, we obtain

$$\frac{\left(1-\underline{1}'\underline{D}^{-1}\underline{\ell}\right)}{\left(\underline{1}'\underline{D}^{-1}\underline{P}+\eta(1-\underline{1}'\underline{D}^{-1}\underline{\ell})\right)}\left[\eta^2+\eta\left\{\frac{\underline{1}'\underline{D}^{-1}(\underline{P}-\underline{Q})-(1-\underline{1}'\underline{D}^{-1}\underline{\ell})^2}{(1-\underline{1}'\underline{D}^{-1}\underline{\ell})}\right\}-\underline{1}'\underline{D}^{-1}\underline{P}\right]=0.$$

Recalling from section 3 that $1-\underline{1}'\underline{D}^{-1}\underline{\ell}=n$, and ignoring the possibility of η having a root equal to $-\underline{1}'\underline{D}^{-1}\underline{P}/n$, we have the equation in η as

(7.4) $$\eta^2+\eta\left(\frac{\underline{1}'\underline{D}^{-1}(\underline{P}-\underline{Q})}{n}-n\right)-\underline{1}'\underline{D}^{-1}\underline{P}=0\ .$$

The equation in ξ is obtained by changing $\underline{P}$ to $\underline{Q}$.

η from (7.4) is obtained as

$$\eta=-\left[\frac{\underline{1}'\underline{D}^{-1}(\underline{P}-\underline{Q})}{2n}-\frac{n}{2}\right]\pm\sqrt{\left[\frac{\underline{1}'\underline{D}^{-1}(\underline{P}-\underline{Q})}{2n}-\frac{n}{2}\right]^2+\underline{1}'\underline{D}^{-1}\underline{P}}\ .$$

Similarly, ξ is obtained as

$$\xi=-\left[\frac{\underline{1}'\underline{D}^{-1}(\underline{Q}-\underline{P})}{2n}-\frac{n}{2}\right]\pm\sqrt{\left[\frac{\underline{1}'\underline{D}^{-1}(\underline{Q}-\underline{P})}{2n}-\frac{n}{2}\right]^2+\underline{1}'\underline{D}^{-1}\underline{Q}}\ .$$

It may be easily verified that the expression under the radical sign in η and ξ is the same. Since both η and ξ have to be positive, we take the positive root in each case, if it exists. After it is assured that a positive value for η and ξ exists, it has to be assured that the elements of $\underline{X}$ (the price indices) and those of $\underline{Y}$ (the quantity indices) have also to be positive. We discuss the question of existence of positive solutions in section 7.

It may be observed that the way the equation (7.4) is derived will hold for any $n>3$. The quadratic equation in η will retain the same form. $\underline{D}_2$ will change to $\underline{D}_{n-1}$, and $\underline{P}$ and $\underline{Q}$ will change respectively to the corresponding vectors with (n-1) elements in each. ξ and η will change respectively to $1+\underline{1}'\underline{X}$ and $1+\underline{1}'\underline{Y}$.

In the next section, $\underline{D}^{-1}\underline{P}$, $\underline{D}^{-1}\underline{Q}$ and $\underline{D}^{-1}(\underline{P}-\underline{Q})$ are expressed in terms of the elements of $(V_{00})^{-1}\underline{V}$. With these reductions, the solutions for the price index vector and the quantity index vector are expressed in terms of the elements of $(V_{00})^{-1}\underline{V}$, and ξ and η.

7.6 The Index Vectors in Terms of the Value Aggregates: Recalling the results from section 3, we write the solutions for $\underline{X}$ and $\underline{Y}$ as

(7.5) $$\underline{X}=\eta^{-1}(\underline{D}^{-1}\underline{P})+\underline{1}$$

(7.6) $$\underline{Y}=\xi^{-1}(\underline{D}^{-1}\underline{Q})+\underline{1}\ .$$

In evaluating $\underline{D}^{-1}\underline{P}$, $\underline{D}^{-1}\underline{Q}$, $\underline{1}'\underline{D}^{-1}(\underline{P}-\underline{Q})$, $\underline{1}'\underline{D}^{-1}\underline{P}$ and $\underline{1}'\underline{D}^{-1}\underline{Q}$, we again refer to the case n=3 to fix ideas. The demonstration is general for any n. We have

(7.7) $$\underline{D}^{-1}\underline{P}=\underline{D}^{-1}\begin{bmatrix}-1 & 0 & +1 & -1 & 0 & +1 & -1 & 0 & +1\\ +1 & -2 & +1 & +1 & -2 & +1 & +1 & -2 & +1\end{bmatrix}\begin{bmatrix}\underline{\gamma}\end{bmatrix},$$

where $\underline{\gamma}=\left[\frac{V_{00}}{V_{00}}, \frac{V_{10}}{V_{00}}, \frac{V_{20}}{V_{00}}, \frac{V_{01}}{V_{00}}, \frac{V_{11}}{V_{00}}, \frac{V_{21}}{V_{00}}, \frac{V_{02}}{V_{00}}, \frac{V_{12}}{V_{00}}, \frac{V_{22}}{V_{00}}\right]'$. The left factor of (7.7) is obtained as

$$\left[\underline{D}^{-1}\underline{\ell} \vdots \ \underline{I}_2 \vdots \ \underline{D}^{-1}\underline{\ell} \vdots \ \underline{I}_2 \vdots \ \underline{D}^{-1}\underline{\ell} \vdots \ \underline{I}_2\right],$$

where $\underline{D}^{-1}\underline{\ell}$ is a column of -1's (from section 3) and $\underline{I}_2$ is an identity matrix of order 2.

From the above,

$$\underline{D}^{-1}\underline{P} = \begin{bmatrix} R_1 - R_0 \\ R_2 - R_0 \end{bmatrix},$$

where R_0, R_1, etc. represent respectively the sum of the elements of the 0th row, 1st row, etc. of $(V_{00})^{-1}\underline{V}$. Similarly,

$$\underline{D}^{-1}\underline{Q} = \begin{bmatrix} C_1 - C_0 \\ C_2 - C_0 \end{bmatrix},$$

where C_0, C_1, etc. represent respectively the sum of the elements of the 0th column, the 1st column, etc. of $(V_{00})^{-1}\underline{V}$.

The elements of $\underline{D}^{-1}\underline{Q}$ may of course be obtained from those of $\underline{D}^{-1}\underline{P}$ by interchanging the suffixes i,j of $\Sigma p_i q_j$. Hence, if η and ξ are known, the price indices and the quantity indices are known in terms of the elements of $(V_{00})^{-1}\underline{V}$.

From the above mode of demonstration, it can be easily seen that the solutions for the price index vector and the quantity index vector are of the same forms for any n>3.

For the calculation of η and ξ, we need to know $\underline{1}'\underline{D}^{-1}\underline{P}$, $\underline{1}'\underline{D}^{-1}\underline{Q}$ and $\underline{1}'\underline{D}^{-1}(\underline{P}-\underline{Q})$ which are given as $\underline{1}'\underline{D}^{-1}\underline{P}=\mathcal{V}-nR_0$, $\underline{1}'\underline{D}^{-1}\underline{Q}=\mathcal{V}-nC_0$, $\underline{1}'\underline{D}^{-1}(\underline{P}-\underline{Q})=n(C_0-R_0)$, where $\mathcal{V}=(V_{00})^{-1}(\underline{1}'\underline{V}\ \underline{1})$, representing the sum of all the elements of $(V_{00})^{-1}\underline{V}$.

The solutions for the price index vector and the quantity index vector are finally presented as

$$(7.8) \qquad \underline{x} = \begin{bmatrix} \eta^{-1}(R_1-R_0)+1 \\ \eta^{-1}(R_2-R_0)+1 \\ \cdots\cdots\cdots\cdots \\ \eta^{-1}(R_{n-1}-R_0)+1 \end{bmatrix}, \quad \underline{y} = \begin{bmatrix} \xi^{-1}(C_1-C_0)+1 \\ \xi^{-1}(C_2-C_0)+1 \\ \cdots\cdots\cdots\cdots \\ \xi^{-1}(C_{n-1}-C_0)+1 \end{bmatrix},$$

where $\eta=\frac{1}{2}[n-(C_0-R_0)]+\sqrt{\mathcal{D}}$, $\xi=\frac{1}{2}[n-(R_0-C_0)]+\sqrt{\mathcal{D}}$, $\mathcal{D}=\left(\frac{C_0-R_0}{2}\right)^2+\frac{n^2}{4}-\frac{n}{2}(C_0+R_0)+\mathcal{V}$. We further note that $\eta-\xi=R_0-C_0$.

If the above solutions are applied to the case n=2, π and κ will be found algebraically to be the same as (2.14), (2.15) or (3.6) (see Chapters Two and Three).

7.7 When Are the Solutions Positive: The quadratic equation in η will have one positive root, if it exists. We may state the conditions as follow:

(7.9) If $\underline{1}'\underline{D}^{-1}\underline{P}$ is positive, η is always real and will have one positive root.

(7.10) If $\underline{1}'\underline{D}^{-1}\underline{P}$ is negative, then for η to be real and positive, we should have

$$\text{(i)} \qquad \left[\frac{\underline{1}'\underline{D}^{-1}(\underline{P}-\underline{Q})}{n} - n\right]^2 \geq 4|\underline{1}'\underline{D}^{-1}\underline{P}|,$$

where | | denotes the absolute value, and further, for a positive root of η to exist, we should have

$$\text{(ii)} \qquad \left(n - \frac{\underline{1}'\underline{D}^{-1}(\underline{P}-\underline{Q})}{n}\right) > 0 .$$

(7.11) If $\underline{D}^{-1}\underline{P}=[(R_1-R_0), (R_2-R_0), \ldots, (R_{n-1}-R_0)]'\geq\underline{0}$, (by this notation we mean that the elements of the vector $\underline{D}'\underline{P}\geq\underline{0}$), then η and the column vector $\underline{X}$ are always positive.

(7.12) If $\underline{D}^{-1}\underline{P}<\underline{0}$, then after it is assured by (7.10) that η is positive, we should have for $\underline{X}$ to be positive,

$$\left(n - \frac{\underline{1}'\underline{D}^{-1}(\underline{P}-\underline{Q})}{n}\right) > \max\left\{|R_1-R_0|, \ldots, |R_{n-1}-R_0|\right\}.$$

Summarizing, we have the following conditions:

(7.13) If all the elements of $\underline{D}^{-1}\underline{P}$ are individually positive, then η and $\underline{X}$ are real and positive.

(7.14) If all the elements of $\underline{D}^{-1}\underline{P}$ are individually negative, then (7.10) and (7.12) should hold for positive solutions to exist.

(7.15) If $\underline{1}'\underline{D}^{-1}\underline{P}$ is positive with some elements of $\underline{D}^{-1}\underline{P}$ as negative, then η is always positive, and $\underline{X}$ is positive, if (7.12) holds for the negative elements.

(7.16) If $\underline{1}'\underline{D}^{-1}\underline{P}$ is negative with some elements of $\underline{D}^{-1}\underline{P}$ as positive, then for η to be real and positive, (7.10) should hold. For the negative elements of $\underline{D}^{-1}\underline{P}$, (7.12) should hold for positive solutions to exist.

The same kinds of conclusions are drawn when $\underline{P}$ is changed to $\underline{Q}$, and correspondingly, η and $\underline{X}$ are changed to ξ and $\underline{Y}$.

If the value aggregates are not purely imaginary, it appears that positive solutions for the price index vector and the quantity index vector will always exist.

7.8 Numerical Illustrations: The data used for these illustrations are arbitrarily chosen. Two sets of data are utilized. It will be noticed that the data in the two illustrations show opposite economic trends in terms of the value aggregates.

The price indices and the quantity indices are shown up to 6 places of decimal, although the value aggregates are recorded only up to one decimal place. We show the price indices and the quantity indices up to 6 places of decimal for illustrative purposes only.

The formulae for the price indices and the quantity indices are drawn from section 6.

Illustration I

$$n=3$$

$$V=\begin{bmatrix} V_{00}(1.0) & V_{01}(0.9) & V_{02}(0.8) \\ V_{10}(1.5) & V_{11}(2.0) & V_{12}(1.4) \\ V_{20}(1.8) & V_{21}(2.2) & V_{22}(1.6) \end{bmatrix} \begin{matrix} \text{Sum} \\ 2.7 \\ 4.9 \\ 5.6 \end{matrix}$$

$$\text{Sum} \quad 4.3 \quad 5.1 \quad 3.8 \quad | \; 13.2$$

$\mathcal{V}=13.2$, $\mathcal{V}-nR_0=5.1$, $\mathcal{V}-nC_0=0.3$

$R_1-R_0=2.2$, $R_2-R_0=2.9$, $C_1-C_0=0.8$, $C_2-C_0=-0.5$, $C_0-R_0=1.6$

Eq. in η: $\eta^2-(1.4)\eta-5.1=0$

$\eta=3.064318$, $\eta^{-1}=0.326337$

Eq. in ξ: $\xi^2-(4.6)\xi-0.3=0$

$\xi=4.664318$, $\xi^{-1}=0.214394$

Price indices

$x_1=\eta^{-1}(R_1-R_0)+1=1.717941$

$x_1x_2=\eta^{-1}(R_2-R_0)+1=1.946377$

$x_2= \quad =1.132971$

Quantity indices

$y_1=\xi^{-1}(C_1-C_0)+1=1.171515$

$y_1y_2=\xi^{-1}(C_2-C_0)+1=0.892803$

$y_2= \quad =0.762093$

Illustration II

$$n=3$$

$$V=\begin{bmatrix} V_{00}(1.00) & V_{01}(0.9) & V_{02}(0.7) \\ V_{10}(0.9) & V_{11}(0.7) & V_{12}(0.6) \\ V_{20}(0.8) & V_{21}(0.6) & V_{22}(0.5) \end{bmatrix} \begin{matrix} \text{Sum} \\ 2.6 \\ 2.2 \\ 1.9 \end{matrix}$$

$$\text{Sum} \quad 2.7 \quad 2.2 \quad 1.8 \quad | \; 6.7$$

$\mathcal{V}=6.7$, $\mathcal{V}-nR_0=-1.1$, $\mathcal{V}-nC_0=-1.4$

$R_1-R_0=-0.4$, $R_2-R_0=-0.7$, $C_1-C_0=-0.5$, $C_2-C_0=-0.9$, $C_0-R_0=0.1$

Eq. in η: $\eta^2-(2.9)\eta+1.1=0$

$\eta=2.451249$, $\eta^{-1}=0.407955$

Eq. in ξ: $\xi^2-(3.1)\xi+1.4=0$

$\xi=2.551249$, $\xi^{-1}=0.391965$

Price indices

$x_1=\eta^{-1}(R_1-R_0)+1=0.836818$

$x_1x_2=\eta^{-1}(R_2-R_0)+1=0.714431$

$x_2= \quad =0.853747$

Quantity indices

$y_1=\xi^{-1}(C_1-C_0)+1=0.804017$

$y_1y_2=\xi^{-1}(C_2-C_0)+1=0.647231$

$y_2= \quad =0.804997$

<u>7.9 The Time Reversal and the Factor Reversal Tests</u>: We demonstrate that the indices presented here satisfy the time reversal test. Since the indices are formulaed as <u>chain indices</u>, such indices have to satisfy the <u>circular test</u> which is a generalization of the time reversal test. That is to say, we shall show that I_{0s}(price) I_{s0}(price)=1 and that I_{0s}(quantity) × I_{s0}(quantity)=1, where I_{ij}, i,j=0,s; s=0,1,...,n-1, indicates the index for the period j compared to the period i.

Again, this property is demonstrated here for n=3. The variables are now shown as π_{01}, $\pi_{01}\pi_{12}$; κ_{01}, $\kappa_{01}\kappa_{12}$; for easy identification.

The four equations are

(7.17) $$V_{00}(-1+\pi_{01}\pi_{12})(1+\kappa_{01}+\kappa_{01}\kappa_{12})=P_1$$

(7.18) $$V_{00}(+1-2\pi_{01}+\pi_{01}\pi_{12})(1+\kappa_{01}+\kappa_{01}\kappa_{12})=P_2$$

(7.19) $$V_{00}(-1+\kappa_{01}\kappa_{12})(1+\pi_{01}+\pi_{01}\pi_{12})=Q_1$$

(7.20) $$V_{00}(+1-2\kappa_{01}+\kappa_{01}\kappa_{12})(1+\pi_{01}+\pi_{01}\pi_{12})=Q_2$$

When reversed in time, the time suffixes would change as

$$\left.\begin{matrix}0\\1\\2\end{matrix}\right\}\Rightarrow\left\{\begin{matrix}2\\1\\0\end{matrix}\right.$$

The suffix 1 does not change. If, therefore, the suffixes 0 and 2 are interchanged, equations (7.17) and (7.18) become

(7.21) $$V_{22}(-1+\pi_{21}\pi_{10})(1+\kappa_{21}+\kappa_{21}\kappa_{10})=P_1^*$$

(7.22) $$V_{22}(+1-2\pi_{21}+\pi_{21}\pi_{10})(1+\kappa_{21}+\kappa_{21}\kappa_{10})=P_2^*,$$

where P_1^* and P_2^* are obtained by interchanging 0 and 2 in the value aggregates. It is noticed that $P_1^*=-P_1$ and that $P_2^*=P_2$. The second component remains unaltered.

If now we substitute as given below

$$\pi_{21}=\frac{1}{\pi_{12}},\quad \pi_{10}=\frac{1}{\pi_{01}}$$

$$\kappa_{21}=\frac{1}{\kappa_{12}},\quad \kappa_{10}=\frac{1}{\kappa_{01}}\quad ,$$

and recall that $\pi_{01}\pi_{12}\kappa_{01}\kappa_{12}=\pi_{02}\kappa_{02}=P_2Q_2/P_0Q_0=\Sigma p_2q_2/\Sigma p_0q_0=V_{22}/V_{00}$, the equations (7.21) and (7.22) change respectively to (7.17) and (7.18) implying that the price indices satisfy the time reversal test or the circular test (when the number of periods is more than 2). The same property will hold with respect to the quantity indices also.

The above demonstration is general. It is to be remembered that the time suffixes will change, in general, in the reverse order as $\{0,1,2,\ldots,(n-2),(n-1)\} \Rightarrow \{(n-1),(n-2),\ldots,2,1,0\}$.

These indices do not satisfy the factor reversal test except when n=2. Theil's Best Linear indices [25] do not satisfy the factor reversal test for any n including 2. However, when n>2, a different definition for the satisfaction of the factor reversal test is perhaps called for. Kloek and DeWit [16] observed that when Theil's analysis was applied to Dutch import and export data, the resulting price and quantity index vectors yielded larger current values. In other words, they noticed an upward bias. We may make a couple of pertinent observations regarding such trends with reference to the indices obtained here from the "factorial approach." The value of $(\xi\eta)$ gives some sort of an estimate of $V=(V_{00})^{-1}\underline{1}'\underline{V}\,\underline{1}$. (It should be remembered in this context that we did not use in our analysis the first of the n^2 possible equations which would have utilized V.) If $(\xi\eta)>V$, we should expect an upward bias. If $(\xi\eta)<V$, the bias will be in the reverse direction. These facts may be verified with reference to the data of the two illustrations which show opposite economic trends.

7.10 Connection with Theil's Procedure: The connection of the factorial approach with Theil's procedure [25], when n=2, was spelled out in Chapter Five. We now extend the analogy when n>2.

In terms of the notations used in this Chapter, $\underline{V}=\underline{P}\,\underline{Q}'$ is the same as $\underline{C}$ in Theil's paper [25]. Theil finds the B. L. price index vector $\underline{p}$, and the quantity index vector $\underline{q}$ by minimizing the sum of squares of the elements of the matrix $\underline{E}$ of cross value discrepancies, where $\underline{E}=\underline{C}-\underline{p}\,\underline{q}'$. In other words, $\underline{p}$ and $\underline{q}$ are such that tr. $(\underline{E}\,\underline{E}')$=tr. $(\underline{E}'\underline{E})$=minimum. The necessary conditions are obtained as

$$(\underline{C}\,\underline{C}'-\underline{p}'\underline{p}\cdot\underline{q}'\underline{q})\underline{p} = 0$$
$$(\underline{C}'\underline{C}-\underline{p}'\underline{p}\cdot\underline{q}'\underline{q})\underline{q} = 0 \ .$$

From the above, it will be clear that $\underline{p}$, $\underline{q}$ are the characteristic vectors of $\underline{C}\,\underline{C}'$ and $\underline{C}'\underline{C}$ respectively, and that $\underline{C}\,\underline{C}'$ and $\underline{C}'\underline{C}$ have the same set of characteristic roots, $\underline{p}'\underline{p}\cdot\underline{q}'\underline{q}=\lambda^2=\lambda$ (say). In order to satisfy that tr. $(\underline{E}\,\underline{E}')$ is the minimum, the characteristic vectors corresponding to the largest root are taken (see Kloek and DeWit [16]).

Let $\underline{A}$ be the normalized form of $\underline{O}_n$, where the elements of the ith row are divided by $S_i^{1/2}$, i=0,1,...,n-1. Also, let $\underline{\tilde{p}}=\underline{A}\ \underline{p}$, $\underline{\tilde{q}}=\underline{A}\ \underline{q}$, $\underline{\tilde{C}}=\underline{A}\ \underline{C}\ \underline{A}'$, $\underline{\tilde{E}}=\underline{A}\ \underline{E}\ \underline{A}'$ where $\underline{A}'$ is the transpose of $\underline{A}$. Under this transformation, the elements of the price index vector $\underline{p}$ and those of the quantity index vector $\underline{q}$ are changed to those of $\underline{\tilde{p}}$ and $\underline{\tilde{q}}$ respectively, while the characteristic roots of $\underline{C}\ \underline{C}'$ and $\underline{C}'\underline{C}$ remain the same as of $\underline{\tilde{C}}\ \underline{\tilde{C}}'$ and $\underline{\tilde{C}}'\underline{\tilde{C}}$. Therefore, in place of the matrix $\underline{C}$, we may use $\underline{\tilde{C}}$. The "mean" and the (n-1) price effects will appear in the first column, while the "mean" and the (n-1) quantity effects will appear in the first row of $\underline{\tilde{C}}$. If the elements of the corresponding $\underline{\tilde{E}}$ matrix are each equated to zero, the 2(n-1) equations appearing in the first column and the first row of $\underline{\tilde{E}}$ will be the same as those utilized in the factorial approach.

Theil's method utilizes the Least Squares of the n^2 cross value discrepancies of $\underline{E}$, whereas in the factorial approach, the cross value discrepancies of 2(n-1) terms of $\underline{\tilde{E}}$ are taken to be exactly *zero*, while not affecting *directly* the remaining cross value discrepancies. We note, in this context, that tr. $(\underline{E}\ \underline{E}')$=tr. $(\underline{\tilde{E}}\ \underline{\tilde{E}}')$ which is minimized in Theil's procedure.

A detailed comparison between the factorial approach and Theil's approach for the case n=2 is provided in Chapter Five. The factorial approach takes, as it were, as much of the substance out of the overall Least Squares procedure as would be necessary to bring the modus operandi meaningfully within easy reach, identifying the procedure with the well defined concepts of a well developed branch of Statistics, *Design of Experiments*.

<u>7.11 Separate Indexes for Price and Quantity and a Remark about the Factorial Indexes</u>: Theil [25] provided the price indices and the quantity indices separately, utilizing separate data, and also the price and quantity indices jointly, considering jointly the price and quantity data. If we apply our analysis separately to the price data or separately to quantity data, we shall get the price index I_{0s}(price) as $\Sigma p_s/\Sigma p_0$, and the quantity index I_{0s}(quantity) as $\Sigma q_s/\Sigma q_0$, for s=1,2,...,n-1. Alternatively, we may also evaluate the separate indices from the joint formulae. For example, if we want the price indices, we may substitute 1 for all q's in the joint formulae. Similarly, if we want the quantity indices, we may substitute 1 for all p's in the joint formulae. The indices will be available in the same forms as above. It is thus observed that an index, whether for price or for quantity, comes out as the ratio of two arithmetic averages of prices and quantities respectively. This phenomenon reveals, in a way, an

implication of the factorial indices. When the price data or the quantity data are considered separately, one may intuitively suggest the forms of the indices as the ratio of two averages. But, then the question arises as to what should be done when the price and quantity data are considered jointly.

CHAPTER EIGHT

AN INTERPRETATION OF A SPECIAL PAIR OF EQUATIONS FROM AMONG THE SIX EMERGING FROM THE FACTORIAL APPROACH

8.0 Chapter Summary: It was indicated in Chapter Three that any pair of equations formed from the four basic equations given by the Factorial Approach, when solved for π and κ, would provide respectively the index of price and the index of quantity. This chapter presents an interesting interpretation of a particular pair out of the six possible pairs of equations. This pair appears to have an importance of its own.

8.1 The Four Basic Equations Leading to the Six Pairs: We reproduce below the four equations which were derived in Chapter Three using the factorial approach.

(8.1) $$\Sigma p_0q_0+\Sigma p_1q_0+\Sigma p_0q_1+\Sigma p_1q_1 = V_0(\pi+1)(\kappa+1)$$

(8.2) $$-\Sigma p_0q_0+\Sigma p_1q_0-\Sigma p_0q_1+\Sigma p_1q_1 = V_0(\pi-1)(\kappa+1)$$

(8.3) $$-\Sigma p_0q_0-\Sigma p_1q_0+\Sigma p_0q_1+\Sigma p_1q_1 = V_0(\pi+1)(\kappa-1)$$

(8.4) $$\Sigma p_0q_0-\Sigma p_1q_0-\Sigma p_0q_1+\Sigma p_1q_1 = V_0(\pi-1)(\kappa-1),$$

where the aggregates Σpq have the usual meanings, $V_0=\Sigma p_0q_0$, and π and κ denote the index of price and the index of quantity, respectively.

As mentioned in Chapter Three, six pairs of equations are possible from the four equations written above, each of which, when solved for π and κ, would provide the indexes for price and quantity. Of the six pairs of equations, the pair with (8.2) and (8.3) is the most important. (See Chapter Three). The true index derived from this pair has all of the desirable properties for the true index of price and the true index of quantity.

The indexes from the pairs {(8.2,8.4), (8.3,8.4), (8.1,8.2), (8.1,8.3)} were discussed in detail in Chapter Three. The interpretation of the indexes from the pair (8.1,8.4) was not made explicit in Chapter Three. It appears that solutions from this pair have an interesting interpretation. Note that like the pair (8.2,8.3), this pair also satisfies the time and the factor reversal tests.

8.2 Demand Dominated Market: Let us recall that equations (8.1) and (8.4) recognize the existence of "subsistence purchases" and the interaction between price and quantity. Neither "the main effect of price," nor "the main effect of quantity" enters into these two equations. When the interaction between price and quantity alone influences consumption, we would consider the market to be "demand dominated," in which case, as it is well known, L_p (Laspeyres' index for price) is greater than P_p (Paasche's index for price), and therefore, correspondingly, L_q (Laspeyres' index for quantity) is greater than P_q (Paasche's index for quantity). Also, in such a situation, the correlation coefficient between price relative and quantity relative is negative (see Allen [1A, pp. 62-65]). Hence, the interpretation of the solutions from this pair would be consistent only with the condition $L_p > P_p$. However, if $L_p < P_p$, the solutions, as shown below, would often be imaginary and hence often be inconsistent.

8.3 The Pair of Equations from (8.1) and (8.4): Let us now turn to equations (8.1) and (8.4). Adding, we get,

$$\pi\kappa = \frac{\Sigma p_1 q_1}{\Sigma p_0 q_0} \quad ,$$

or

(8.5)
$$\kappa = \frac{\Sigma p_1 q_1}{\pi \Sigma p_0 q_0} \quad .$$

Substituting (8.5) in (8.1), we have

(8.6)
$$\pi^2 - \pi(L_p + L_q) + P_p L_q = 0,$$

where $P_p L_q$ is written for $\Sigma p_1 q_1 / \Sigma p_0 q_0$. (Also $P_p L_q = L_p P_q$.)

Solving for π, we have

(8.7)
$$\pi = \frac{L_p + L_q}{2} \pm \sqrt{\left(\frac{L_p + L_q}{2}\right)^2 - P_p L_q} \quad .$$

The same equation would be obtained also for κ.

We have, therefore, to provide a rule as to which of the two solutions would be relevant for π, and which for κ.

8.4 Discussion of the Situation when $L_p < P_p$: We now show that if $L_p < P_p$, the expression within the radical sign of (8.7) may often be negative. Three cases will arise.

(i) $L_p < P_p$ and $L_p = L_q$. The expression within the radical sign of (8.7) is

$$(L_p + L_q)^2 - 4P_p L_q = 4L_p^2 - 4P_p L_p = 4L_p(L_p - P_p) \Rightarrow \text{negative}.$$

(ii) $L_p < P_p$ and $L_p > L_q$. The above $\Rightarrow P_p > L_p > L_q$. The expression within the radical sign of (8.7) is negative, if

$$[(L_p + L_q)/2]^2 < P_p L_q.$$

This condition implies that the Arithmetic Mean of L_p and L_q is less than the Geometric Mean of P_p and L_q. This may often be true in situation (ii).

(iii) $L_p<P_p$ and $L_p<L_q$.

$$L_p<P_p \Leftrightarrow L_q<P_q. \text{ Also, } P_pL_q = L_pP_q.$$

The above $\Rightarrow P_q>L_q>L_p$. The expression within the radical sign of (8.7) is negative, if

$$[(L_p+L_q)/2]^2 < P_pL_q = L_pP_q.$$

This condition implies that the Arithmetic Mean of L_p and L_q is less than the Geometric Mean of P_q and L_p. This may often be true in situation (iii).

Thus, when $L_p<P_p$, the solutions from equation (8.7) may often be imaginary.

8.5 Resolution of the Ambiguity Between π and κ: When $L_p>P_p$,

$$[(L_p+L_q)/2]^2-P_pL_q = \tfrac{1}{4}[(L_p+L_q)^2-4P_pL_q]$$

$$(8.8) \qquad = \tfrac{1}{4}[(L_p-L_q)^2+4L_q(L_p-P_p)] \Rightarrow \text{positive.}$$

The ambiguity for π and κ may be resolved by associating π with the positive square root of (8.8), and κ with the negative square root. By this rule, $\pi\to L_p$ and $\kappa\to L_q$, as $L_p\to P_p$, as may be seen from (8.8).

8.6 Remarks: Since the indexes satisfy the time reversal and the factor reversal tests, a question naturally arises if this pair could also be used to provide the "true index." If, as enunciated, κ is set equal to 1 in equation (8.4), the necessary condition to determine q_1 equivalent to q_0, would be obtained as

$$\Sigma p_0q_0-\Sigma p_1q_0-\Sigma p_0q_1+\Sigma p_1q_1 = 0,$$

or equivalently, in terms of notations used before,

$$(8.9) \qquad V_{00}-V_{10}-V_{01}+V_{11} = 0.$$

Condition (8.9) implies that the interaction term is zero, which, in turn, implies that either $\kappa=1$ or $\pi=1$, or both $\pi=1$ and $\kappa=1$ simultaneously. This condition, therefore, does not lead to a unique condition, as visualized in the enunciation of the "true index" through the "factorial approach." Thus, the only pair left for finding the "true index" is the pair from equations (8.2) and (8.3).

8.7 Natural Indices Given by Vogt: Vogt [25A] studied the index number problem in the two-situation case in the 2n-dimensional quantity-price space, and obtained some known index number formulae by evaluating the

Divisia line integral on certain paths in this space. Of special interest are what he calls the "natural indices" obtained by evaluating the Divisia line integral on the straight line connecting the base point, $\underline{r}_0=(\underline{p}_0,\underline{q}_0)$, and the observed point, $\underline{r}_1=(\underline{p}_1,\underline{q}_1)$, where the price and the quantity vectors are represented respectively by $\underline{p}$ and $\underline{q}$. The price index P_{01} and quantity index Q_{01} are developed as

(8.10)
$$P_{01}^{(C)}=\exp\int_{t_0}^{t_1}\frac{\dot{\underline{p}}(\tau)\underline{q}(\tau)}{\underline{p}(\tau)\underline{q}(\tau)}\,d\tau\rightarrow P_{01}^{(nat)}=\exp\int_0^1\frac{(\underline{q}^0+t(\underline{q}^1-\underline{q}^0))(\underline{p}^1-\underline{p}^0)}{(\underline{q}^0+t(\underline{q}^1-\underline{q}^0))(\underline{p}^0+t(\underline{p}^1-\underline{p}^0))}\,dt$$
$$Q_{01}^{(C)}=\exp\int_{t_0}^{t_1}\frac{\underline{p}(\tau)\dot{\underline{q}}(\tau)}{\underline{p}(\tau)\underline{q}(\tau)}\,d\tau\rightarrow Q_{01}^{(nat)}=\exp\int_0^1\frac{(\underline{q}^1-\underline{q}^0)(\underline{p}^0+t(\underline{p}^1-\underline{p}^0))}{(\underline{q}^0+t(\underline{q}^1-\underline{q}^0))(\underline{p}^0+t(\underline{p}^1-\underline{p}^0))}\,dt\ .$$

The indices are dependent on the path C in the 2n-space, which runs from $\underline{r}_0$ to $\underline{r}_1$ along the path $(\underline{p}(t),\underline{q}(t))$ parametrized by the time parameter $t\epsilon[t_0,t_1]$. The indices $P_{01}^{(C)}$ and $Q_{01}^{(C)}$, evaluated on the straight line connecting $\underline{r}_0$ and $\underline{r}_1$ are called by Vogt [25A] the "natural indices," being given by

(8.11)
$$P_{01}^{(nat)}=\begin{cases}\sqrt{\frac{V_{11}}{V_{00}}}\left(\frac{V_{10}+V_{01}+\sqrt{D}}{V_{10}+V_{01}-\sqrt{D}}\right)^{\frac{V_{10}-V_{01}}{2\sqrt{D}}}, & D>0\\ \sqrt{\frac{V_{11}}{V_{00}}}\exp\frac{V_{10}-V_{01}}{V_{10}+V_{01}}, & D=0\\ \sqrt{\frac{V_{11}}{V_{00}}}\exp\left(\frac{V_{10}-V_{01}}{\sqrt{-D}}\operatorname{arctg}\frac{\sqrt{-D}}{V_{10}+V_{01}}\right), & D<0\ ,\end{cases}$$

where $V_{ij}=\underline{p}^i\underline{q}^i$, i,j=0,1, and $D=(V_{10}+V_{01})^2-4V_{00}V_{11}$. The "natural" quantity indices are similarly evaluated, which, however, may be obtained from $P_{01}^{(nat)}$ by interchanging the suffixes i,j of V_{ij}. We shall refer to "D" as the discriminant.

<u>8.8 Connection of Vogt's work with the Special Pair of Equations Emerging from the Factorial Approach</u>: Equations (8.1) and (8.4) appear to have an implied connection with the integrand in (8.10) leading to Vogt's natural indices. In the above discussion concerning this pair of equations (see

Banerjee [9A])[8], we used the following expression entering into the solutions for π and κ,

(8.12) $$[(L_p+L_q)^2-4P_pL_q] = E \text{ (say)},$$

as a discriminant to demonstrate that $L_p<P_p \Rightarrow E<0$ (in some situations), and that $L_p>P_p \Rightarrow E>0$. Since D and E are related as

(8.13) $$D = V_{00}\, E,$$

we shall have (i) $D<0 \Leftrightarrow E<0$, (ii) $D>0 \Leftrightarrow E>0$, and (iii) $D=0 \Leftrightarrow E=0$.

8.9 Some Results on the Discriminant and an Interpretation of Vogt's Natural Indices:

Result I

$$E<0 \Rightarrow (L_p+L_q)^2<4P_pL_q=4L_pL_q+4L_q(P_p-L_p)$$

$$\Rightarrow \left(\frac{L_p-L_q}{2}\right)^2<L_q(P_p-L_p) \Rightarrow L_p<P_p.$$

Result II

$E>0 \Rightarrow [(L_p+L_q)/2]^2 > P_pL_q$. When $L_p=L_q$, $E>0 \Rightarrow L_p>P_p$. When either $L_p<L_q$ or $L_p>L_q$, L_p may be either $>P_p$ or $<P_p$ in both situations. On the other hand, when $L_p>P_p$, it is shown in Banerjee [9A] that $E>0$.

Result III

$E=0 \Rightarrow (L_p-L_q)^2+4L_q(L_p-P_p)=0 \Rightarrow$ either $L_p<P_p$, or $L_p=P_p$ with $L_p=L_q \Rightarrow$ $L_p=P_p=L_q=P_q=(V_{11}/V_{00})^{\frac{1}{2}}$, and $V_{10}=V_{01}$.

It is thus observed that Vogt's "natural indices" will apply to the "supply-dominated" market when $D<0$ ($L_p<P_p$). When $D=0$, the "natural indices" will apply either to the "supply-dominated" market, or $P_{01}^{(nat)}=Q_{01}^{(nat)}=L_p=P_p=L_q=P_q=(V_{11}/V_{00})^{\frac{1}{2}}$. However, when $D>0$, the natural indices will apply in general to both "supply-dominated" and "demand-dominated" markets.

8.10 A Few Additional Remarks: As mentioned above the price index $\pi \to L_p$ and the quantity index $\kappa \to L_q$, as $L_p \to P_p$. This result appears to be in agreement with the findings of Vogt. In the factorial approach, we used, in the spirit of the Divisia Indices, the identities, $V_{00}=P_0Q_0$, $V_{10}=P_1Q_0$, $V_{01}=P_0Q_1$, $V_{11}=P_1Q_1$, where P represents a general price level, and Q represents a measure of physical volume of goods. With these assumptions, the difference $(V_{11}-V_{00})$ was expressible as the sum of "the main effect of price"

---

[8]This note has later been slightly amended.

and "the main effect of quantity." The "main effects" are the same as understood in the context of a 2^2-factorial design, where the "price" and the "quantity" are the factors. This result also agrees in spirit with the Divisia Indices. In the next chapter, a closer connection is traced between the "factorial indexes" and the Divisia Indices.

CHAPTER NINE

AN INTERPRETATION OF THE FACTORIAL INDEXES IN THE LIGHT OF DIVISIA INTEGRAL INDEXES

9.0 Chapter Summary: This chapter provides an interpretation of the "factorial indexes" in the light of the Divisia Integral Indexes.

9.1 The Divisia Integral Indexes: The Divisia Integral Index for price, P(t), and the Divisia Integral Index for quantity, Q(t), are defined continuously on a path over time t such that

$$V(t) = P(t)\ Q(t) \tag{9.1}$$

is satisfied for all t, where V(t) represents the value at time t. The fulfillment of restraint (9.1) implies the fulfillment of the factor reversal test. Such indexes are also required to satisfy, if possible, the circular test. (For a recent account of the Divisia Indexes, see Allen [1A]). As the problem in the present context concerns two discrete points in time corresponding to t=0, and t=1, the circular test would reduce to the time reversal test. From (9.1), setting t=0, t=1, we have

$$\frac{V(1)}{V(0)} = \frac{P(1)Q(1)}{P(0)Q(0)} \tag{9.2}$$

which implies that the value index is equal to the product of the price index and the quantity index.

In determining the Divisia indexes from the Integral approach, we may think of two distinct procedures, Procedure I (without logarithmic differentiation) and Procedure II (with logarithmic differentiation).

Let the prices and quantities of n commodities in the period 0 (base period) and the period 1 (period of comparison), defined in the positive domain of the 2n-price-quantity space, be given as $(\underline{p}^0,\underline{q}^0)$ and $(\underline{p}^1,\underline{q}^1)$, respectively, where a "sub-bar" is used to denote a vector. In terms of the notations used earlier, we have $\Sigma p_0q_1=\underline{p}^0\underline{q}^1$, $\Sigma p_1q_0=\underline{p}^1\underline{q}^0$, $\Sigma p_0q_1=\underline{p}^0\underline{q}^1$, $\Sigma p_1q_1=\underline{p}^1\underline{q}^1$.

Procedure I

From (9.1), we have

$$d(P(t)Q(t))=d(V(t))=d(\Sigma p_i(t)q_i(t))=\Sigma q_i(t)dp_i(t)+\Sigma p_i(t)dq_i(t)$$

$$\Rightarrow \underline{p}^1\underline{q}^1-\underline{p}^0\underline{q}^0 = \int_C \underline{q}(t)d\underline{p}(t) + \int_C \underline{p}(t)d\underline{q}(t), \tag{9.3}$$

$$= I_p+I_q$$

where C indicates the contour taken by $[p_i(t),q_i(t)]$ between the end points, t=0 and t=1, and I_p and I_q denote the results of integration relevant, respectively, to change in price and change in quantity. The L.H.S. of (9.3) is invariant, being the integral of an exact differential, while the R.H.S. is the sum of two non-invariant parts. From (9.3), we have

$$(9.4)\qquad \begin{aligned} V(1)-V(0) &= V_0\left(\frac{P(1)Q(1)}{P(0)Q(0)} - 1\right) \\ &= V_0(\pi\kappa-1) = I_p+I_q, \end{aligned}$$

where π and κ are the required price and quantity indexes. One may seek to evaluate π and κ from (9.4). Alternatively, one may also adopt Procedure II, described below, to determine π and κ.

Procedure II

Taking the logarithmic differential and integrating along the contour C from the point t=0 to the point t=1, we have

$$(9.5)\qquad \begin{aligned} &\ln(P(1)Q(1)) - \ln(P(0)Q(0)) \\ &= \ln\left(\frac{P(1)Q(1)}{P(0)Q(0)}\right) = \ln(\pi)+\ln(\kappa) = \int_C \frac{\underline{q}(t)d\underline{p}(t)}{\underline{p}(t)\underline{q}(t)} + \int_C \frac{\underline{p}(t)d\underline{q}(t)}{\underline{p}(t)\underline{q}(t)} \\ &= J_p + J_q . \end{aligned}$$

Here also, the invariant L.H.S. of (9.5) breaks into two non-invariant parts, J_p and J_q.

9.2 Indexes Under the Two Procedures: In Procedure II which is commonly associated with the name of Divisia in evaluating the Divisia Integral Indexes, one takes $\pi=\exp J_p$, and $\kappa=\exp J_q$ as a solution for π and κ from equation (9.5) which is a single equation in two variables appearing as a sum of two logarithms. The justification of this term-by-term allocation of the sum on the R.H.S. to π and κ on the L.H.S. is made to lie in the assumption that the components J_p and J_q coming, respectively, from change in price and change in quantity should be attributable, respectively, to the price index and the quantity index. (See Allen [1A], Samuelson and Swamy [20], and Vogt [25A].) In view of this situation, one wonders if it were possible to suggest a different set of solutions for π and κ, dependent on the possibility that each of J_p and J_q could perhaps be taken as a function of both π and κ.

While equation (9.5) provides a decomposition of the type mentioned above, equation (9.4) in Procedure I, which is also a single equation in two variables, does not provide a similar easily identifiable break down to determine π and κ. In Procedure I which we shall adopt to show the connection with the factorial indexes, each of I_p and I_q will come out as a function of both π and κ, satisfying equation (9.4).

9.3 Evaluation of the Integrals Along Three Different Contours by Procedure I: Vogt [25A] adopted Procedure II to determine the price index π and the quantity index κ on several different contours. As mentioned above, since the "factorial indexes" are related to Procedure I, we shall adopt Procedure I for the evaluations, and shall concentrate only on three different contours, two of which are step paths and the third, a straight line, as indicated below:

(i) C_1: $(\underline{p}^0,\underline{q}^0)\rightarrow(\underline{p}^0,\underline{q}^1)\rightarrow(\underline{p}^1,\underline{q}^1)$ (step path)

(ii) C_2: $(\underline{p}^0,\underline{q}^0)\rightarrow(\underline{p}^1,\underline{q}^0)\rightarrow(\underline{p}^1,\underline{q}^1)$ (step path)

(iii) C_3: straight line from $(\underline{p}^0,\underline{q}^0)$ to $(\underline{p}^1,\underline{q}^1)$, where a point on the line is represented by

$$\left.\begin{array}{l}\underline{p}(t)=\underline{p}^0+t(\underline{p}^1-\underline{p}^0)\\ \underline{q}(t)=\underline{q}^0+t(\underline{q}^1-\underline{q}^0)\end{array}\right\},\ t\in[0,1].$$

The above paths are marked in Diagram I, "each axis symbolically representing an n-dimensional subspace" (see Vogt [25A]). The results of integration are indicated in Table I. The price and quantity components resulting from integration in each path are shown by the subscripts p and q, respectively. For example, $C_{1\cdot p}$ indicates the result of integration along C_1 when price varies, being given by

$$C_{1\cdot p}=\int_{C_1}\underline{q}(t)d\underline{p}(t).$$

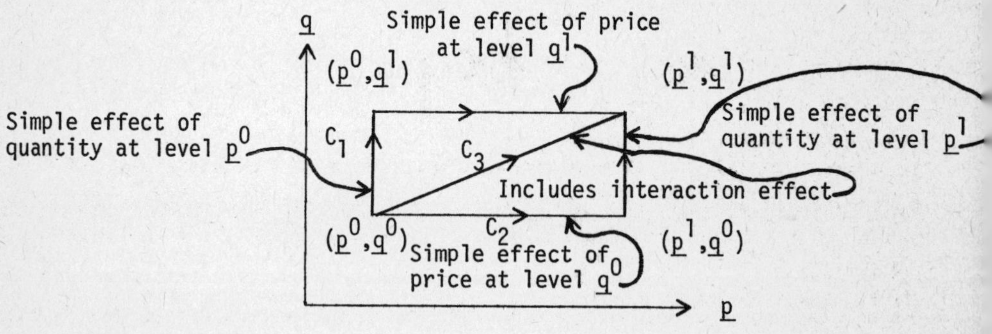

Diagram I: Three Different Contours for the Divisia Integrals

Table 1: Results of Integration Along Different Paths

C_1		C_2		C_3	
$C_{1\cdot p}$	$C_{1\cdot q}$	$C_{2\cdot p}$	$C_{2\cdot q}$	$C_{3\cdot p}$	$C_{3\cdot q}$
$\underline{p}^1\underline{q}^1-\underline{p}^0\underline{q}^1$ $=\Sigma p_1q_1-\Sigma p_0q_1$ →Simple effect of price at level $\underline{q}^1$.	$\underline{p}^0\underline{q}^1-\underline{p}^0\underline{q}^0$ $=\Sigma p_0q_1-\Sigma p_0q_0$ →Simple effect of quantity at level $\underline{p}^0$.	$\underline{p}^1\underline{q}^0-\underline{p}^0\underline{q}^0$ $=\Sigma p_1q_0-\Sigma p_0q_0$ →Simple effect of price at level $\underline{q}^0$.	$\underline{p}^1\underline{q}^1-\underline{p}^1\underline{q}^0$ $=\Sigma p_1q_1-\Sigma p_1q_0$ →Simple effect of quantity at level $\underline{p}^1$.	$(\underline{p}^1\underline{q}^0-\underline{p}^0\underline{q}^0)$ $+\frac{1}{2}(\underline{p}^1\underline{q}^1-\underline{p}^1\underline{q}^0$ $-\underline{p}^0\underline{q}^1+\underline{p}^0\underline{q}^0)$ $=P_s+PQ/2$, where P_s represents the simple effect of price at level $\underline{q}^0$ and PQ/2 represents interaction ⇛ price effect, if the two components could be combined.	$\underline{p}^0\underline{q}^1-\underline{p}^0\underline{q}^0$ $+\frac{1}{2}(\underline{p}^1\underline{q}^1-\underline{p}^1\underline{q}^0$ $-\underline{p}^0\underline{q}^1+\underline{p}^0\underline{q}^0)$ $=Q_s+PQ/2$, where Q_s represents the simple effect of quantity at level $\underline{p}^0$ and PQ/2 represents interaction ⇛ quantity effect, if the two components could be combined.

9.4 Formation of Pairs of Equations to Determine the Price and Quantity Indexes: The six pairs of equations, referred to earlier, to determine π and κ as given by the factorial approach, can now be related to six different pairs of equations formed from the component parts, $C_{1\cdot p}$, $C_{1\cdot q}$, $C_{2\cdot p}$, $C_{2\cdot q}$, $C_{3\cdot p}$ and $C_{3\cdot q}$. The building up of equations (3.5.2) and (3.5.3) of Chapter Three proceeds as follows: We combine $C_{1\cdot p}$ with $C_{2\cdot p}$, and $C_{1\cdot q}$ with $C_{2\cdot q}$, and take an average of the two in each case, as shown below:

(9.6) $$\tfrac{1}{2}[C_{1\cdot p}+C_{2\cdot p}] = \tfrac{1}{2}[-\Sigma p_0q_0+\Sigma p_1q_0-\Sigma p_0q_1+\Sigma p_1q_1]$$

(9.7) $$\tfrac{1}{2}[C_{1\cdot q}+C_{2\cdot q}] = \tfrac{1}{2}[-\Sigma p_0q_1-\Sigma p_1q_0+\Sigma p_0q_1+\Sigma p_1q_1].$$

The combinations go, respectively, in the direction of price, and in the direction of quantity. The directions are marked by arrows in Diagram I. Each of $C_{1\cdot p}$ and $C_{2\cdot p}$ represents a "simple effect" of price, and each of $C_{1\cdot q}$ and $C_{2\cdot q}$, a "simple effect" of quantity. Such "simple effects" are the same as understood in the language of Design of Experiments in the context of a 2^2-factorial experiment. The average of $C_{1\cdot p}$ and $C_{2\cdot p}$ represents the main effect of price, and the average of $C_{1\cdot q}$ and $C_{2\cdot q}$, the main effect of quantity.

Consistent with restraint (9.1) which should hold at every point of any contour under consideration, we write $V_{00}=\Sigma p_0q_0=P_0Q_0$, $\Sigma p_1q_0=P_1Q_0$, $\Sigma p_0q_1=P_0Q_1$, $V_{11}=\Sigma p_1q_1=P_1Q_1$, with $\pi=P_1/P_0$, $\kappa=Q_1/Q_0$. Equations (9.6) and (9.7) would then reduce to the equations (3.5.2) and (3.5.3) (see Chapter Three), with the R.H.S. expressed in terms of π and κ. It will be noticed that the sum of (3.5.2) and (3.5.3) satisfies equation (9.4), being equal to $V_{00}(\pi\kappa-1)$, where $V_0=V_{00}$. This is the first pair. How the remaining five pairs of equations may be formed is indicated below:

(i) Average of C_1 and C_2

(a) $\frac{1}{2}(C_{1\cdot p}+C_{2\cdot p})$
(b) $\frac{1}{2}(C_{1\cdot q}+C_{2\cdot q})$
⟹ Equations (3.5.2) and (3.5.3) Price effect and Quantity effect.

(ii) C_3

(a) P_s+Q_s
(b) $PQ/2+PQ/2=PQ$
⟹ Equations (3.5.1) and (3.5.4) Mean and Interaction effect.

That it so implies will be clear, if we add $3\underline{p}^0\underline{q}^0+\underline{p}^1\underline{q}^1$ to both sides in (iia) in C_3.

(iii) Combine $C_{1\cdot p}$ and $C_{3\cdot p}$

(a) $C_{1\cdot p}+P_s$
(b) $PQ/2$
⟹ Equations (3.5.2) and (3.5.4) Price effect and Interaction effect.

(iv) Combine $C_{2\cdot q}$ and $C_{3\cdot q}$

(a) $C_{2\cdot q}+Q_s$
(b) $PQ/2$
⟹ Equations (3.5.3) and (3.5.4) Quantity effect and Interaction effect.

(v) Combine $C_{1\cdot q}$ and $C_{3\cdot p}$

(a) $C_{1\cdot q}$
(b) two parts of $C_{3\cdot p}$ combined
⟹ Equations (3.5.1) and (3.5.2) Mean and Price effect.

(vi) Combine $C_{2\cdot p}$ and $C_{3\cdot q}$

(a) $C_{2\cdot p}$
(b) two parts of $C_{3\cdot q}$ combined
⟹ Equations (3.5.1) and (3.5.3) Mean and Quantity effect.

Like pair (i), the pair (ii) also satisfies equation (9.4). π and κ, in turn, satisfy the factor reversal and the time reversal tests, but for reasons stated earlier in Chapter Three and Chapter Eight, pair (ii) could not be utilized for finding the "true" indexes. Although the remaining pairs of equations do not satisfy the factor reversal or the time reversal test, the indexes coming from solutions of those pairs of equations are also meaningful. Such indexes include Laspeyres', Paasche's and Marshall-Edgeworth's price and quantity indexes (see Chapter Three).

CHAPTER TEN

A COMPARISON OF THE CONSTANT-UTILITY TRUE INDEX AND THE TRUE INDEX OBTAINED THROUGH THE FACTORIAL APPROACH

10.0 Chapter Summary: This Chapter provides an empirical and an algebraic comparison between the formula for "true " Index of Cost of Living (true CLI) (synonymously referred to in this Chapter as constant-utility price index,or economic price index,or simply as true index of price), given by the Factorial Approach (FA) on one hand, and, on the other, the formula for the constant-utility index of price given by the Klein-Rubin (Geary-Stone) form of the utility function and the formula for the true CLI emerging from quadratic approximation of the utility function as given by Wald. The agreement is demonstrated to be remarkable.

The discussion starts with the mention of a couple of well known facts concerning the status of the constant-utility true index of price indicating the background against which the Factorial True Indexes are to be viewed. Some of the results referred to in the earlier Chapters are repeated here by way of a review to bring together the relevant facts.

10.1 Introduction: We recall that in the economic theory of price indices, as envisaged in the economic theory of consumer choice in the set-up of maximization of ordinal utility, an economic price index (synonymously referred to in this Chapter as a constant-utility price index, or the true index of Cost of Living,or simply as the true index of price) is the ratio of the minimum costs of a given level of utility (a given level of living) in two price situations. It is well known that in the economic theory a formula for such a price index, which we shall often refer to as the true index of Cost of Living (true CLI), cannot be presented unless we assume a specific form of the utility function. However, such a formula can be provided, as we have seen in Chapter Three, without assuming any form of the utility function, if we adopt the Factorial Approach (FA).

This Chapter presents an algebraic and empirical comparison between the true CLI obtained through the FA and two other well known constant utility price indices, one of which is based on the Klein-Rubin [15C] (Geary-Stone [13A,23A]) form of the utility function, and the other, on quadratic approximation of the utility function as given by Wald [26].

10.2 Status of Constant-Utility Price Indices under the Economic Theory: As referred to earlier, it is possible to present a formula of the constant-utility index of price when the utility function is known. Some forms (or models) of the utility function have, at times, been specified and tried, and the parameters of the utility function statistically estimated to present such an index number formula. The errors involved in the estimation of the parameters, which are sometimes too many in number, make the indexes subject to a "decided disadvantage" (see Theil [25A, pp. 134-138]). On top of it, the formula, that is finally presented, is tied in with the form of the utility function.

10.3 Two Different Indexes for the Same Price Comparison: When the utility function is not specified, we can, at best, provide some limits to the "true" indexes. It is known that the true index of price $I_{01}(q_0)$ for the period 1 (the period of comparison) compared to the period 0 (the base period), based on the optimal consumption q_0 specifying the corresponding level of utility at the base period, is different from the true index of price $I_{01}(q_1)$, based on the optimal consumption q_1 specifying the corresponding level of utility at the period of comparison.

$I_{01}(q_0)$ and $I_{01}(q_1)$ are bounded above and bounded below, respectively, by Laspeyres' price index L_p and Paasche's price index P_p, as shown below.

$$P_p=(\Sigma p_1q_1/\Sigma p_0q_1) \quad < \quad I_{01}(q_1)$$

$$I_{01}(q_0) \quad < \quad (\Sigma p_1q_0/\Sigma p_0q_0)=L_p.$$

Paasches' price index	Two different true indexes	Laspeyres' price index

It thus transpires that, if and when the form of a utility function is assumed, two different constant-utility price index formulae will emerge for the same price comparison. In view of this situation, one wishes that both these indexes be the same. Work of Konüs [17], Haberler [14], Staehle [23] and Wald [26], among others, suggests that they had been looking for a point q* on the indifference map of the period 1, which would be equivalent in utility corresponding to the point q_0 in the period 0 with a convenient modus operandi such that $I_{01}(q_0)=I_{01}(q^*)$. Should the equivalence, $I_{01}(q_0)=I_{01}(q^*)$, happen, the true indexes being the same should lie between L_p and P_p. In this context, Sir Roy Allen [1A, p. 70] observes: "The practical thought was always that though the Laspeyres' and Paasche bounds applied in theory to separate true index numbers, there should be a strong presumption that any one true index could be pinned down between both bounds."

10.4 Plato's Heaven: In order to achieve the condition, $I_{01}(q_0)=I_{01}(q^*)$, it is put forward by Samuelson and Swamy [20] that the only way left is to use a homothetic form of the utility function which, as we know, satisfies such a condition. But, then again, homothetic preferences impose a serious restriction on the form of the utility function, thus detracting from the general acceptability of the index. Also, a true index formula can be presented only when a specific form of the homothetic utility function is assumed. Forms of such utility functions are infinitely many in number. This being so, Samuelson and Swamy [20, p. 568] write "....there is an uncountable infinity of different index number formulas, which dooms Fisher's search for the ideal one. *It does not exist even in Plato's heaven*". Such a situation emerges from the fact that one has to depend on the form of a utility function.

10.5 The Basic Equations from the Factorial Approach: We reproduce below, from Chapter Three, the following four basic equations given by the FA.

(10.1) $+\Sigma p_0q_0+\Sigma p_1q_0+\Sigma p_0q_1+\Sigma p_1q_1 = V_{00}(\pi+1)(\kappa+1)$

(10.2) $-\Sigma p_0q_0+\Sigma p_1q_0-\Sigma p_0q_1+\Sigma p_1q_1 = V_{00}(\pi-1)(\kappa+1)$

(10.3) $-\Sigma p_0q_0-\Sigma p_1q_0+\Sigma p_0q_1+\Sigma p_1q_1 = V_{00}(\pi+1)(\kappa-1)$

(10.4) $+\Sigma p_0q_0-\Sigma p_1q_0-\Sigma p_0q_1+\Sigma p_1q_1 = V_{00}(\pi-1)(\kappa-1)$.

The aggregates Σpq have the usual meanings, $V_{00}=\Sigma p_0q_0$, and π and κ denote respectively the index of price and the index of quantity. It may be recalled that it is possible to form four orthogonal linear functions from four entities (the four aggregates) in an infinite number of ways, but only the above four have identification with the factorial effects and the interaction in the context of a 2^2-Factorial Experiment, with price and quantity as the factors, and the periods 0 and 1 as the levels. Equations (10.1) - (10.4) represent, respectively, the general effect (Mean) (interpreted as what may be due to "subsistence purchases"), the effect of price, the effect of quantity and the interaction effect between price and quantity.

Six pairs of equations would emerge from the above four equations, any pair of which, when solved for π and κ, would provide different index number formulae for price and quantity including Laspeyres', Paasche's and Marshall-Edgeworth's indexes (see Chapter Three). Although the pairs, {(10.1) and (10.4)} and {(10.2) and (10.3)}, would both provide indexes satisfying the factor and the time reversal tests, the pair, {(10.2) and (10.3)}, was chosen, for reasons stated in Chapter Three and Chapter Eight, for the purpose of determining the true indexes. *We recall that a point q^* in the period 1 is taken as equivalent in utility to a point q_0 in the period 0, if the quantity index for q^* compared to q_0 is unity.* This condition is in keeping with the rationale of the economic theory. If two points of consumption lie on the same indifference surface, the "true" index of quantity (index of real consumption) of one point compared to the other will be unity, and the true index of price between the two price situations will be the ratio of the value aggregates of the two points.

10.6 The Condition Giving the True Index of Price: Since the point q* is in the period 1, we shall refer to it as q_1. The required q_1 is obtained by setting $\kappa=1$ in (10.3). The resulting condition, which implies, in the language of Design of Experiments, that the effect of quantity be zero, is given by

(10.5) $$V_{11}-V_{10}+V_{01}-V_{00} = 0$$

where $V_{11}=\Sigma p_1q_1$, $V_{10}=\Sigma p_1q_0$, $V_{01}=\Sigma p_0q_1$, $V_{00}=\Sigma p_0q_0$.

As mentioned in Chapter Three, condition (10.5) is similar to the condition, $V_{11}V_{01}=V_{10}V_{00}$, worked out by Frisch [13] in his double expenditure method. Multiplication there takes the place of addition in (10.5). A logarithmic transformation of the condition given by Frisch will provide the same form of the linear function as in (10.5). Again, as referred to in Chapter Three, Frische's condition may be interpreted as $F_q=1$, where F_q is Fisher's ideal index of quantity. If we use $F_q=1$ in the ideal price index of Fisher, the price index comes out as the ratio of the two expenditures (value index). This interpretation of Frische's condition has an interest in the context of our present discussion, because we take a certain quantity index as unity.

Condition (10.5) has also a similarity with Konüs conditions as worked out and clarified by Staehle [23, pp. 183-187] in providing limits (an L_p and a P_p for a price index) to the two price indexes, one based on q_0 and the other based on q_1, where q_0 and q_1 represent the two optimal points in the two periods. The conditions are expressed as

$$\text{(i)}\quad \Sigma p_0q_1-\Sigma p_0q_0 = 0, \qquad \text{(ii)}\quad \Sigma p_1q_1-\Sigma p_1q_0 = 0.$$

The above two conditions represent respectively Laspeyres' and Paasche's quantity indexes equated to unities. Condition (10.5) is the sum of the above two conditions, and may be considered to be an alignment of the two, giving us one condition for one price index between the two periods with L_p and P_p as the bounds. These facts would reveal that condition (10.5), derived from a different approach, makes sense, as it bears a close analogy with conditions derived from economic theory (Frisch) and utility concept (Konüs).

Condition (10.5) has also an interpretation in terms of the standards of living (utilities) in the two periods (see Chapter Three).

<u>10.7 The True Index of Price</u>: Combining (10.5) with (10.2), the true index of price (true CLI) is obtained (see Chapter Three) as

$$(10.6) \qquad \pi = \frac{V_{11}}{V_{00}} = \frac{P_p(L_p+1)}{(P_p+1)} = I_{01}^{price}\,(q_0) \quad \text{(say)}$$

where L_p and P_p denote respectively the Laspeyres' and Paasche's index of price. It has been shown (Chapter Three) that the true index (10.6) lies between L_p and P_p. The expression (10.6) is obtained from (10.5), but the fact that V_{11}/V_{00} is equal to π comes from (10.2) and (10.5). If the suffixes (0,1) in (5) are interchanged, the true index of price, $I_{01}^{price}\,(q_1)$, will be the same.

That is,

$$(10.7) \qquad I_{01}^{price}\,(q_0) = I_{01}^{price}\,(q_1).$$

Demonstration of (10.7) is straightforward, as shown below.

In demonstrating (10.7), we have again to remind ourselves that this q_1 is not the equilibrium point in the period 1. It is q* in the period 1, which we seek to find as being equivalent to the point q_0 in the period 0. As q* is in the period 1, we write it as q_1.

Equation (10.2) represents the effect of the price p_1 in the period 1, compared to the price p_0 in the period 0, and equation (10.3) represents the effect of the quantity q_1 in the period 1, compared to the quantity q_0 in the period 0. We now reverse the directions of the price effect and the quantity effect. In other words, we find the effect of the price p_0 in the period 0, compared to the price p_1 in the period 1, and the effect of the quantity q_0 in the period 0, compared to the quantity q_1 in the period 1. These effects may be obtained by interchanging the suffixes 0 and 1.

Equations (10.2) and (10.3) will then change respectively to

$$(10.2)^* \qquad -\Sigma p_1q_1+\Sigma p_0q_1-\Sigma p_1q_0+\Sigma p_0q_0 = V_{11}(\pi'-1)(\kappa'+1)$$
$$(10.3)^* \qquad -\Sigma p_1q_1-\Sigma p_0q_1+\Sigma p_1q_0+\Sigma p_0q_0 = V_{11}(\pi'+1)(\kappa'-1),$$

where $\pi'=P_0/P_1$, $\kappa'=Q_0/Q_1$.

The true index of price $I_{10}^{price}\,(q_1)$ will be obtained by taking $\kappa'=1$. Notice that the suffixes of the index I are now changed to (1,0) from (0,1).

Substituting $\kappa'=1$ in (10.2)* and (10.3)*, we have

(10.2)** $$-\Sigma p_1q_1+\Sigma p_0q_1-\Sigma p_1q_0+\Sigma p_0q_0 = 2V_{11}(\pi'-1)$$

(10.3)** $$-\Sigma p_1q_1-\Sigma p_0q_1+\Sigma p_1q_0+\Sigma p_0q_0 = 0.$$

Adding (10.2)** and (10.3)**, and dividing both sides by $2V_{11}=2\Sigma p_1q_1$, we have

$$-\left(1 - \frac{\Sigma p_0q_0}{\Sigma p_1q_1}\right) = (\pi'-1)$$

$$\Rightarrow \pi' = \Sigma p_0q_0/\Sigma p_1q_1 = V_{00}/V_{11}.$$

V_{00}/V_{11} is now obtained from (10.3)**:

$$-V_{11}-V_{01}+V_{10}+V_{00} = 0$$

$$\Rightarrow -1 - \frac{V_{01}}{V_{11}} + \frac{V_{00}}{V_{11}}\left(1 + \frac{V_{10}}{V_{00}}\right) = 0$$

$$\Rightarrow -1 - \frac{1}{P_p} + \frac{V_{00}}{V_{11}}(L_p+1) = 0$$

$$\Rightarrow \frac{V_{00}}{V_{11}} = \frac{(P_p+1)}{P_p(L_p+1)} = I_{10}^{price}\ (q_1).$$

The above result is the reciprocal of (10.6). Hence,

$$I_{01}^{price}\ (q_1) = \frac{P_p(L_p+1)}{(P_p+1)} = I_{01}^{price}\ (q_0).$$

<u>10.8 The True Index of Quantity</u>: Similarly, the true index of quantity is obtained from (10.2) and (10.3) by setting $\pi=1$ in (10.2). The relevant condition is then obtained as

(10.8) $$V_{11}-V_{01}+V_{10}-V_{00} = 0.$$

From (10.8), we obtain the true index of quantity as

(10.9) $$\kappa = \frac{V_{11}}{V_{00}} = \frac{P_q(L_q+1)}{(P_q+1)} = I_{01}^{quantity}\ (p_0) \quad \text{(say)}$$

where L_q $(=\Sigma p_0q_1/\Sigma p_0q_0)$ and P_q $(=\Sigma p_1q_1/\Sigma p_1q_0)$ denote respectively Laspeyres' and Paasche's quantity indexes. That the true index of quantity lies between L_q and P_q may be shown as follows. The true index κ may be expressed in the following two equivalent forms:

$$\text{(i)}\quad \kappa = \frac{P_q(L_q+1)}{(P_q+1)}\ ;$$

$$\text{(ii)}\quad \kappa = \frac{L_q(1 + \frac{1}{L_q})}{1 + \frac{1}{P_q}}\ .$$

Let $L_q>P_q$. Then from (i) $\kappa>P_q$, and from (ii) $L_q>\kappa$. Thus, $L_q>\kappa>P_q$. Again, let $L_q<P_q$. Then, from (i) $P_q>\kappa$, and from (ii) $\kappa>L_q$. Thus, $P_q>\kappa>L_q$. Hence, κ lies between L_q and P_q. (Incidentally, the proof that the true index of price lies between L_p and P_p can also be shown on similar reasoning (see Chapter Three).)

In the case of quantity index also, we shall have

$$I_{01}^{\text{quantity}}(p_0) = I_{01}^{\text{quantity}}(p_1).$$

<u>10.9 Reduction of Wald's True Index and the True Index from the Factorial Approach in Terms of the Coefficients of the Engel Curves</u>: Let the linear Engel curves C_0 (period 0) and C_1 (period 1) be given by the following equations. (See Wald [26]):

(10.10) $$C_0:\ q_0^i=\alpha_0^i V+\beta_0^i,\quad C_1:\ q_1^i=\alpha_1^i V+\beta_1^i,\quad (i=1,2,\dots,n),$$

where the symbols have the usual meanings and n represents the number of commodities consumed. Let

$$\sum_{i=1}^{n}\alpha_j^i\, p_k^i = a_{jk} \text{ and } \sum_{i=1}^{n}\beta_j^i\, p_k^i = b_{jk},\ (j,k=0,1).$$

Then, $a_{jj}=1$, $b_{jj}=0$, $(j=0,1)$. Also, $\sum_{i=1}^{n} p_0^i q_0^i=V_{00}$, $V_{01}=a_{10}V_{11}+b_{10}$, $V_{10}=a_{01}V_{00}+b_{01}$, $\sum_{i=1}^{n} p_1^i q_1^i=V_{11}$.

In terms of the coefficients of the Engel Curves, the true index of price (true CLI) (see Chapter Three), utilizing (10.5), is obtained as

(10.11) $$I_{01}^{\text{price}}(q_0) = \frac{1+a_{01}}{1+a_{10}} + \frac{1}{V_{00}}\ \frac{(b_{01}-b_{10})}{(1+a_{10})}.$$

The true index (10.11) is more restricted than (10.6). In (10.11), we restrict ourselves to the linearity of demand functions. For comparison with the other true indexes which are based on linear demand functions, we shall use (10.11).

Wald's formula in terms of the coefficients of the Engel Curves (see Wald [26]) is given by

(10.12) $$W = \sqrt{\frac{a_{01}}{a_{10}}} + \frac{1}{V_{00}}\ \frac{b_{01} - \frac{b_{10}}{a_{10}}\sqrt{a_{01}\, a_{10}}}{1+\sqrt{a_{10}\, a_{01}}}.$$

The interested reader may refer to Tintner [25B, p. 60-61] where an empirical application of Wald's method is discussed. (Incidentally, the ipso facto derivation of Wald's formula is presented in Banerjee [9B]).

10.10 Klein-Rubin (Geary/Stone) Form of the Utility Function and the Constant-Utility Index of Price: The Klein-Rubin [15C] [or Geary/Stone, 13A, 23A] form of the ordinal utility function may be written as

$$(10.13) \qquad U = \prod_i (q^i - c^i)^{d^i}, \; d^i>0, \; \Sigma\, d^i = 1, \; c^i>0, \; (q^i - c^i)>0 \; .$$

Maximizing U subject to the budget restraint, $\Sigma p^i q^i = y$, the demand functions in quantities are obtained as

$$(10.14) \qquad q_0^i = c^i + \frac{d^i}{p_0^i}(y_0 - \Sigma p_0^i c^i), \quad q_1^i = c^i + \frac{d^i}{p_1^i}(y_1 - \Sigma p_1^i c^i),$$

and the constant-utility index of price is obtained (see also Allen [1A]) as

$$(10.15) \qquad I_{01}(y) = \left(\frac{h_0}{y}\right)\left(\frac{h_1}{h_0}\right) + \left(1 - \frac{h_0}{y}\right)\left(\frac{g_1}{g_0}\right),$$

where $h_0 = \Sigma p_0^i c^i$, $h_1 = \Sigma p_1^i c^i$, $g_0 = \prod_i \left(\frac{p_0^i}{d^i}\right)^{d^i}$, and $g_1 = \prod_i \left(\frac{p_1^i}{d^i}\right)^{d^i}$.

Expression (10.15) is recognized as the weighted average of two price indexes, one of which is based on "necessaries" and the other on "luxuries." The ratio, g_1/g_0, of (10.5) reduces to

$$(10.16) \qquad G = \prod_i \left(\frac{p_1^i}{p_0^i}\right)^{d^i}, \; d^i>0, \; \Sigma\, d^i = 1.$$

10.11 Reduction of the Factorial-Approach True Index to a Comparable Form: The expression (10.11), when reduced in terms of the coefficients of (10.14), takes the form,

$$(10.17) \qquad \left(\frac{h_0}{y}\right)\left(\frac{h_1}{h_0}\right) + \left(1 - \frac{h_0}{y}\right)\left(\frac{1+A}{1+B}\right),$$

where $y = V_{00}$, $A = \Sigma_i\, d^i(p_1^i/p_0^i)$ and $B = \Sigma_i\, d^i(p_0^i/p_1^i)$. We shall write $F = (1+A)/(1+B)$.

The expressions (10.17) and (10.15) are the same except for the difference between F and G. The similarity in form between (10.15) and (10.17) is noticeable. F and G denote respectively the indexes which would be obtained under homothetic preferences. Comparison of (10.17) and (10.15), therefore, rests on the comparison of the indexes under homothetic preferences, which appear as component parts of (10.17) and (10.15). G, A and B represent respectively the Geometric Mean (GM), the Arithmetic Mean (AM) and the reciprocal of the Harmonic Mean (HM) of the price relatives. We have F=(1+AM)/(1+1/HM)=HM(1+AM)/(1+HM). Since, AM>HM, the above implies that F>HM. Again, F=AM(1+1/AM)/(1+1/HM), and this implies AM>F, which, with the above, implies AM>F>HM. Thus, F also lies between the same limits as G does. Hence, F and G should be close to one another. In other words, the constant-utility price index obtained from the Klein-Rubin (Geary/Stone) form of the utility function should be close to the true index of price obtained from the FA. Whatever the difference between F and G, the difference in the overall index will be less pronounced, since the difference is multiplied by the associated weight which is a fraction. An empirical comparison is provided in section (10.14) to indicate the extent of agreement between F and G.

We note that if the prices have changed from the period 0 to the period 1 by the same proportion λ, λ will be the value of both the indexes, F and G.

10.12 Wald's True Index and the Factorial True Index in Comparable Forms:

Wald's [26] true index (10.12) is based on permissibility to approximate the utility function by a quadratic polynomial in the region of interest. The quadratic utility function will be assumed to be of the following form,

$$U(\underline{X}) = 2\underline{H}'\underline{X} - \underline{X}'\underline{A}\underline{X} \tag{10.18}$$

where $\underline{X}$ stands for the column vector of the quantities consumed, $\underline{H}$ for the column vector of constants and $\underline{A}$ is assumed to be a positive definite (symmetric) matrix of constants. Expression (10.18) represents the most general form of a second degree polynomial in the quantities, except for a constant term which may be ignored, as U(X) represents the form of an ordinal utility function. Maximizing (10.18) subject to the budget restraint, $\underline{p}'\underline{X}$=E, where $\underline{p}$ stands for the column vector of price and E for the expenditure, the demand functions, in quantities, take the following form:

$$\underline{X} = \frac{[E-\underline{H}'\underline{A}^{-1}\underline{p}]}{\underline{p}'\underline{A}^{-1}\underline{p}} \; \underline{A}^{-1}\underline{p} + \underline{A}^{-1}\underline{H} \; . \tag{10.19}$$

We can find $\underline{X}_0$, the quantities consumed in the period (0), by changing $\underline{p}$ to $\underline{p}_0$ and E to E_0, and also $\underline{X}_1$, the quantities consumed in the period (1), by changing $\underline{p}$ to $\underline{p}_1$ and E to E_1. Expression (10.19) has the same form of (10.10). Comparing the coefficients, we find

$$a_{01} = \frac{\underline{p}_0' \underline{A}^{-1} \underline{p}_1}{\underline{p}_0' \underline{A}^{-1} \underline{p}_0}, \quad a_{10} = \frac{\underline{p}_1' \underline{A}^{-1} \underline{p}_0}{\underline{p}_1' \underline{A}^{-1} \underline{p}_1}, \quad b_{01} = \underline{H}'\underline{A}^{-1}\underline{p}_1 -$$

$$\frac{\underline{H}'\underline{A}^{-1} \underline{p}_0}{\underline{p}_0'\underline{A}^{-1} \underline{p}_0} \underline{p}_1' \underline{A}^{-1} \underline{p}_0, \quad b_{10} = \underline{H}'\underline{A}^{-1}\underline{p}_0 - \frac{\underline{H}'\underline{A}^{-1} \underline{p}_1}{\underline{p}_1'\underline{A}^{-1} \underline{p}_1} \underline{p}_1' \underline{A}^{-1} \underline{p}_0.$$

Writing $\underline{p}_0'\underline{A}^{-1}\underline{p}_1=C_{01}=C_{10}=\underline{p}_1'\underline{A}^{-1}\underline{p}_0$, $\underline{p}_0'\underline{A}^{-1}\underline{p}_0=C_{00}$, $\underline{p}_1'\underline{A}^{-1}\underline{p}_1=C_{11}$, $\underline{H}'\underline{A}^{-1}\underline{p}_0=D_0$ and $\underline{H}'\underline{A}^{-1}\underline{p}_1=D_1$, the true index of price (10.11) obtained from the FA reduces to

$$(10.20) \qquad (\frac{D_0}{V_{00}})(\frac{D_1}{D_0}) + (1 - \frac{D_0}{V_{00}})(\frac{C_{00}+C_{01}}{C_{01}+C_{11}})(\frac{C_{11}}{C_{00}}),$$

where $V_{00}=E_0$. The expression (10.20) is recognized, again, as the weighted average of two price indexes. We shall write

$$(10.21) \quad K=[(C_{00}+C_{01})/(C_{01}+C_{11})](C_{11}/C_{00})=(1+C_{01}/C_{00})/(1+C_{01}/C_{11}).$$

Wald's true index (10.12), when reduced in terms of the coefficients noted above, takes the following form:

$$(10.22) \qquad (\frac{D_0}{V_{00}})(\frac{D_1}{D_0}) + (1 - \frac{D_0}{V_{00}}) \sqrt{\frac{C_{11}}{C_{00}}}\,.$$

We shall write

$$(10.23) \qquad L = (C_{11}/C_{00})^{\frac{1}{2}}.$$

Similarity in form between (10.20) and (10.22) is, again, noticeable. It will further be noticed that the difference in Wald's true index and the true index emerging from the FA lies in the difference between K and L. K and L denote respectively the indexes which would be obtained under homothetic preferences. Thus, here again, difference between (10.20) and (10.22) rests on the difference between the indexes obtained under homothetic preferences, which appear as component parts of the indexes (10.20) and (10.22).

If $\underline{A}$ is positive definite, (and so is $\underline{A}^{-1}$), then there exists a nonsingular matrix $\underline{P}$ such that $\underline{p}_1'\underline{A}^{-1}\underline{p}_1=\xi'\xi$, $\underline{p}_0'\underline{A}^{-1}\underline{p}_0=\eta'\eta$, $A^{-1}=PP'$, $\underline{p}_1'\underline{A}^{-1}\underline{p}_0=\underline{p}_0'\underline{A}^{-1}\underline{p}_1=\underline{\xi}'\underline{\eta}$, where $\xi=\underline{P}'\underline{p}_1$ and $\eta=\underline{P}'\underline{p}_0$. Substituting these values in (10.21), we find

$$(10.24) \qquad K = \frac{1 + \frac{\xi'\eta}{\sqrt{(\xi'\xi)(\eta'\eta)}}(L)}{1 + \frac{\xi'\eta}{\sqrt{(\xi'\xi)(\eta'\eta)}}(\frac{1}{L})} = \frac{1 + \text{Cos}\theta\ L}{1 + \text{Cos}\theta\ \frac{1}{L}},$$

where θ is the angle between the vectors ξ and η.

If θ is small, K=L, as the first approximation. Such a situation will obtain when the vectors $\underline{p}_1$ and $\underline{p}_0$ are not too far apart.

Also, if the elements of the price vectors change by the same proportion λ, Cosθ will be 1, and λ will be the value of the indexes, K and L.

It is thus evident that Wald's true index should be close to the true index obtained from the FA as a first approximation. An empirical comparison between K and L is provided in section (10.14).

In the next section, we provide a comparison between Wald's true index and the constant-utility index arising from the Klein-Rubin (Geary/Stone) form of the utility function. This is done by reducing Wald's true index in terms of the coefficients of the demand functions in the Klein-Rubin (Geary/Stone) form. Such a comparison should, therefore, provide also an indirect comparison between Wald's true index and the true index obtained from the FA, because the latter has already been compared in section (10.11) with the constant-utility index emerging from the Klein-Rubin (Geary/Stone) form.

<u>10.13 A Comparison of Wald's True Index and the Constant-Utility Index Obtained from the Klein-Rubin (Geary/Stone) Form</u>: Equating the corresponding coefficients of (10.10) and (10.14), Wald's true index (10.22) reduces to

$$\left(\frac{h_0}{y}\right)\left(\frac{h_1}{h_0}\right) + \left(1 - \frac{h_0}{y}\right)W, \text{ where}$$

$$W=(C_{11}/C_{00})^{\frac{1}{2}}=[\sum_i d^i(p_1^i/p_0^i)/\sum_i d^i(p_0^i/p_1^i)]^{\frac{1}{2}}=(A/B)^{\frac{1}{2}}=[(AM)(HM)]^{\frac{1}{2}}.$$

G, being the Geometric Mean, lies between the AM and the HM. W also lies between the AM and the HM. Thus, this analysis indicates that Wald's true index and the constant-utility index from the Klein-Rubin (Geary/Stone) form should be close. It was indicated earlier that the true index obtained from the FA should be close to the constant-utility index obtained from the Klein-Rubin (Geary/Stone) form. Thus, all the three should be close to one another. An indication of the extent of agreement on an empirical basis is provided in section (10.14).

Here again, if the individual prices change by the same proportionality λ, λ will be the value of the index W.

<u>10.14 An Empirical Comparison of the True Indexes</u>: Table (1) is designed to provide an empirical comparison among the true index from the FA, the constant-utility index from the Klein-Rubin (Geary/Stone) form and Wald's true index based on quadratic approximation of the utility function. It has

been demonstrated in the preceding sections that these indexes are algebraically the same except for those component parts, appearing in these indexes, which would have been obtained under "homothetic preferences."

Comparison between the true index from the FA and the constant-utility index from the Klein-Rubin (Geary/Stone) form is made by comparing F and G which represent respectively the component parts referred to above. For this comparison, the true index from the FA is reduced to the Klein-Rubin (Geary/Stone) form (see sections (10.10) and (10.11)). Again, comparison between Wald's true index and the constant-utility index from the Klein-Rubin (Geary/Stone) form is made by comparing W and G. In this latter comparison, Wald's true index is reduced to the Klein-Rubin (Geary/Stone) form. (See section (10.13)).

Price vectors have been generated with 5 elements, 10 elements and 15 elements.[9] The elements of $\underline{p}_0$ have been obtained by adding 1 to a random error from the normal distribution, $N[0,(.15)^2]$, while the elements of $\underline{p}_1$, obtained by adding 1·2 to a random error from the same normal distribution. The arbitrary prices in the period 1 are designed to show some random fluctuations beyond the scaling factor of 1·2. The intention is just to have a set of random prices of this nature, and not to suggest any "model" for the price behavior.

The parameters d^i have been randomly generated and later normalized to the condition $\Sigma\, d^i=1$.

The computations of F, G and W have been replicated a number of times. Only the first seven in the serial order are recorded in table (1). The table indicates that there is, in general, a close agreement between F and G, and also between G and W. The agreement goes up to the third decimal place in general.

Table (2) shows the comparison between the true index from the FA and Wald's true index based on quadratic approximation. Here, both forms of the indexes are reduced to a common form in terms of the coefficients of demand functions given by a quadratic utility function. The difference in the two indexes would come from the difference between K and L which would have been obtained under "homothetic preferences." (See section (10.12)).

---

[9]I am grateful to Dr. J. R. Moore of Aberdeen Proving Ground, Md. for some of the numerical calculations of this section.

Table (1): Agreement Among the True Index From the Factorial Approach, Wald's True Index and the Constant-Utility Index From the Klein-Rubin (Geary/Stone) Form, All Based on the Klein-Rubin (Geary/Stone) Form.

Values of the symbols

G	F	W
The price vector with 5 elements		
1.312176	1.312761	1.312139
1.249272	1.249685	1.249037
1.332897	1.333110	1.332924
1.117224	1.117488	1.116545
1.079442	1.079994	1.079603
1.191559	1.195400	1.192482
1.294637	1.295313	1.294693
The price vector with 10 elements		
1.286136	1.287033	1.286203
1.159153	1.159916	1.159072
1.159964	1.161572	1.160401
1.282167	1.288929	1.284524
1.226760	1.229659	1.227438
1.195740	1.196901	1.195469
1.244777	1.246451	1.244562
The price vector with 15 elements		
1.082868	1.088063	1.082480
1.246165	1.247939	1.245628
1.242163	1.246858	1.243356
1.216167	1.218703	1.217013
1.239043	1.241628	1.239109
1.302178	1.306471	1.301721
1.256576	1.259682	1.257786

Table (2): Agreement Between the True Index From the Factorial Approach and Wald's True Index, Both Based on General Form of a Quadratic Utility Function.

Values of the Different Symbols

Price Vector $\underline{p}_0$	Price Vector $\underline{p}_1$	K	L	Cosθ
2.12	3.62	3.183983	3.185440	0.9991
1.23	1.89	2.043734	2.044386	0.9991
0.19	1.20	0.652230	0.646058	0.9567
1.26	0.58	1.480944	1.487899	0.9764
0.86	1.02	0.482498	0.477445	0.9707
1.01	1.01	1.015404	1.016633	0.8634
1.29	2.13	1.285928	0.958719	-0.7474

It is shown in section (10.12) that agreement between K and L would depend upon the magnitude of Cosθ. The agreement will be close, if θ is small, or, equivalently, if Cosθ is near 1. Such a condition will be satisfied, if the price vector $\underline{p}_1$ is close to the price vector $\underline{p}_0$, or the elements of the price vectors are nearly proportional.

The price vectors in this comparison are chosen to have 7 elements as shown in table (2). With a purpose, the price vectors $\underline{p}_0$ and $\underline{p}_1$ are so chosen that these are not as close as were considered in table (1). The elements of the price vectors are shown in table (2). Positive definite matrices A of dimensions 7×7 have been randomly generated.

Seven different values of K, L, and Cosθ are indicated in table (2), each for the same price vectors, $\underline{p}_0$ and $\underline{p}_1$. These values are typical. Values as extreme as shown in the last row may also occur occasionally.

Agreement between K and L is still close, except that as shown in the last row of the table. A part of the possible agreement appears to have been masked by the rounding errors involved in the computation of the quadratic forms. Roughly speaking, the vector $\underline{p}_1$ shows an increase over $\underline{p}_0$ by about 98 percent on the average. But, the indexes shown under L (Wald) in this table do not reflect this order of the increase, except the one shown in the second row. This might raise a question on the appropriateness for the random choice of $\underline{A}$ itself, the elements of which have interrelated economic interpretations in the context of the utility. (Incidentally, the agreement is quite close in the second row).

In table (1), where the comparison is made by way of the Klein-Rubin (Geary/Stone) form, the agreement between these two indexes is found to be remarkably close.

10.15 Remarks: The true index (10.6) obtained from the Factorial Approach is of a general nature, and its calculation depends only upon L_p and P_p. It will be applicable to demand functions which are not necessarily linear, whereas the constant-utility index obtained from the Klein-Rubin (Geary/Stone) form and Wald's true index are based on utility functions which provide linear demand functions. Since the latter two indexes are inherent in econometric literature, it was felt that there was a necessity for a comparison showing how the true index obtained from the FA stands vis-a-vis such well known true indexes obtained from specified forms of the utility function. The agreement revealed in the above comparisons suggests that the true index from the FA, which assumes no specified form, and is dependent only on L_p and P_p, should be acceptable for all practical purposes.

ABSTRACT

This article provides a comprehensive review of the "factorial approach" providing the "true index" of cost of living (economic price index). Most of this presentation is a reproduction of earlier work of the author except for some technical details and a renewed emphasis on some aspects of the problem. Starting with the derivation of Stuvel's new indexes with which the "factorial approach" is connected, this article spells out in full the "factorial approach" model (or the "least squares" model) and brings the potential of the methodology to bear upon several problems of connected interest including the construction of multidimensional indexes. It is shown in detail how the "factorial approach" provides the basis of a joint formulation for constructing the "true index" of cost of living (economic price index) and the "true index" of quantity (economic quantity index). Simultaneously, it is also shown how such a formulation can help in splitting the National Income of a country (or "value change") into two independent components, one due to price and the other due to quantity. The numerical calculations of the economic indices and the decomposition of the National Income are eventually illustrated in a statistical table. In the sequel, a connection of the factorial indexes with Theil's best linear unbiased indexes is traced, and a generalization of Stuvel's averaging procedure worked out providing additional index number formulae. The methodology is extended also to provide index number formulae of price and quantity for an arbitrary number of periods (or geographical units) with numerical illustrations. The connection of the factorial approach with the Divisia Integral Indexes is made more explicit, and finally, an algebraic and empirical comparison is made between the factorial "true index" of price and the constant-utility "true index" of price given by the Klein-Rubin (Geary/Stone) form of the utility function and the "true index" of price based on quadratic approximation of the utility function as given by Wald. The agreement is demonstrated to be remarkable.

Zusammenfassung

Dieser Artikel gibt einen umfassenden Überblick über den faktoriellen Ansatz, der zum "richtigen Index" für die Lebenshaltungskosten führt. Der überwiegende Teil des Dargestellten greift frühere Arbeiten des Autors auf, wobei formeltechnische Änderungen eingearbeitet und einige Aspekte des Problems erneut betont wurden. Mit der Ableitung von Stuvels Indizes, mit denen der faktorielle Ansatz verbunden ist, wird begonnen; danach folgt eine ausführliche Darlegung dieses faktoriellen Modellansatzes (oder des Kleinst-Quadrate-Modells). Hierbei werden die Möglichkeiten dieser Methode im Hinblick auf ähnlich gelagerte Probleme einschließlich der Konstruktion eines mehrdimensionalen Index deutlich. Es wird in allen Einzelheiten gezeigt, daß der faktorielle Ansatz die gemeinsame Grundlage für die Konstruktion eines "richtigen Index der Lebenshaltungskosten" (Preisindex) und eines "richtigen Mengenindex" bildet.

Gleichzeitig wird gezeigt, daß eine solche Darstellung geeignet ist, das Volkseinkommen oder seine Bewertungsänderungen in zwei unabhängige Komponenten zu zerlegen. Eine Komponente ist dabei preis-, die andere mengenbestimmt. Die numerischen Ergebnisse der ökonomischen Indizes und die Zerlegung des Volkseinkommens werden von Fall zu Fall durch statistische Tabellen erläutert.

Nachfolgend wird eine Verbindung zwischen den faktorisierten Indizes mit den Theilschen besten unverzerrten Indizes hergestellt. Ferner wird eine Verallgemeinerung der Stuvelschen Durchschnittsbildungen vorgenommen, um additive Index-Formeln zu gewinnen.

Diese Methodik wird ausgedehnt, um Index-Formeln für Preise und Mengen einer beliebigen Anzahl von Perioden (oder geographische Einheiten) herzuleiten und wiederum numerisch zu verdeutlichen.

Der Zusammenhang des Faktor-Ansatzes mit den Gesamt-Indizes (Divisia) wird deutlich gemacht. Abschließend wird ein algebraischer und numerischer Vergleich zwischen dem faktoriell "richtigen Preisindex" und dem "richtigen Preisindex" bei konstantem Nutzen vorgenommen. Dieser basiert auf der von Klein-Rubin (Georg/Stone) eingeführten

Form der Nutzenfunktion und auf einem "richtigen Preisindex", der auf der Waldschen quadratischen Approximation der Nutzenfunktion beruht. Die Übereinstimmung kann als bemerkenswert bezeichnet werden.

RESUME

Cet article donne une vue d'ensemble de la méthode factorielle qui permet de construire un "indice vrai" du coût de la vie (indice des prix).

Ce travail à l'exception de détails techniques et de la mise au point de certains aspects du problème est la reproduction de précèdents articles de l'auteur. Partant du calcul des nouveaux indices de Stuvel qui est relié à la "méthode factorielle", cet article fignole la méthode de "l'approche factoriel" (ou modèle des "moindres carrés" et applique à divers problèmes les possibilités de cette méthodologie, notamment la contraction des indices multidimensionnels. On montre en détail comment la méthode factorielle donne les bases d'une construction simultanée de "l'indice vrai" du côut de la vie (indice des prix) et de l'indice vrai des quantités (indice économique de quantité).

En même temps, on montre comment une telle formulation peut permettre de partager le Revenu National d'un pays en 2 composantes indépendantes dont l'une est due à la variation des prix et l'autre à la variation des quantités. Le calcul numérique des indices économiques et la décomposition du revenu national sont illustrés par un tableau statistique. Pour finir, on montre une relation entre les indices factoriels et les meilleurs indices linéaires sans biais de Theil et on élabore une généralisation de la méthode de Stuvel qui donne de nouveaux nombres indices. La méthodologie est aussi étendue en vue d'obtenir des formules de nombres indices de prix et de quantité pour un nombre arbitraire de périodes (ou d'unités géographiques) On explicite la liaison entre la méthode factorielle et l'indice monétaire de Divisia et on compare "l'indice vrai" des prix et "l'indice vrai" d'utilité constante donné par la forme de Klein-Rubin de la fonction d'utilité (Geary-Stone ainsi que l'indice vrai des prix basé sur l'approximation de la fonction d'utilité que donne Wald.
On montre que ces différents indices sont remarquablement voisins

REFERENCES

[1] Afriat, S. N: "The Theory of International Comparisons of Real Incomes and Prices," in J.D. Daly, ed., International Comparisons of Prices and Output, Nat. Bur. Econ. Res. Stud. in Income and Wealth, Vol. 37 New York (1972), 15-94.

[2] Allen, R.G.D: "The nature of indifference curves," Rev. Econ. Stud. (1934), 110-121.

[3] Banerjee, K. S: "A factorial approach to construction of true cost of living index and its application in studies of changes in national income," Sankhyā, Series A, Vol. 23, (1961), 297-304.

[4] Banerjee, K. S: "A unified statistical approach to the index number problem," Econometrica, Vol. 29, No. 4, (1961), 591-601.

[5] Banerjee, K. S: "Best linear unbiased index numbers and index numbers obtained through a factorial approach," Econometrica, Vol. 31, No. 4, (1963), 712-718.

[6] Banerjee, K. S: "A generalization of Stuvel's index number formulae," Econometrica, 27, No. 4 (1959), 676-678.

[7] Banerjee, K. S: "Index Numbers for factorial effects and their connection with a special kind of irregular fractional plans of factorial experiments," Jour. Am. Stat. Assoc., 58, (1963), 497-508.

[8] Banerjee, K. S. and Federer, W. T: "On a special subset giving an irregular fractional replicate of a 2^n-factorial experiment," J.R.S.S., Series B, 29(1967), 292-299.

[9] Banerjee, K. S: Cost of Living Index Numbers: Practice, Precision and Theory, Marcel Dekker Inc., New York, 1975.

[10] Bechhofer, R. E: "A multiplicative model for analyzing variances which are affected by several factors," Jour. Am. Stat. Assoc., 55(1960), 245-64.

[11] Fisher, F. M. and Shell, K: The economic theory of price indices, Academic Press, New York (1972).

[12] Fisher, I: The Making of Index Numbers. Boston: Houghton-Mifflin, 1927. 3rd ed., rev. reprinted 1967 by Augustus M. Kelly, New York.

[13] Frisch, R: "Annual survey of general economic theory: The problem of index numbers." Econometrica, IV, No. 1, (1936), 1-38.

[14] Haberler, G: Der Sinn der Indexzahlen, Tubingen, 1927.

[15] Hicks, J. R: A Revision of Demand Theory, Oxford (1956).

[16] Kloek, R., and DeWit, G. D: "Best Linear and Best Linear Unbiased Index Numbers," Econometrica, 29, No. 4, (1961), 602-616.

[17] Konüs, A. A: "The problem of the true index of the cost of living," Econometrica, Vol. 7, No. 1, (1939) 10-29.

[18] Malmquist, S: "Index Numbers and indifference surfaces," Trabajos de Estadistica (1953), 4, 209-242.

[19] Pollak, R. A: "The Theory of the Cost of Living Index," unpublished paper, Univ. Pennsylvania, June, 1971.

[20] Samuelson, P. A. and Swamy, S: "Invariant Economic Index Numbers and Canonical Duality: Survey and Synthesis," Amer. Econ. Rev. 64, (1974), 566-593.

[21] Samuelson, P. A: "Foundations of Economic Analysis," Cambridge, Massachusetts, Harvard University Press, 1947.

[22] Siegel, I. H: "The generalized 'ideal' index number formula," Jour. Am. Stat. Assoc., 40(1945), 520-23.

[23] Staehle, H: "A development of the economic theory of price index numbers," The Review of Economic Studies, (1935), 163-188.

[24] Stuvel, G: "A new index number formula." Econometrica 26, No. 1, (1957), 123-131.

[25] Thiel, H: "Best linear index numbers of prices and quantities," Econometrica, Vol. 28, No. 2, (1960), 464-480.

[26] Wald, A: "A new formula for the index of cost of living." Econometrica, 7, No. 4, (1939), 319-331.

[27] Wisniewski, J. K: "Extension of Fisher's formula number 353 to three or more variables," Journ. Am. Stat. Assoc., 26(1931), 62-5.

[28] Wold, H. O. and L. Jureen: Demand Analysis, New York, John Wiley & Sons, 1953.

ADDITIONAL REFERENCES[10]

[1A] Allen, R.G.D: Index numbers in theory and practice, London, The Macmillan Company (1975).

[9A] Banerjee, K. S: "On the factorial approach providing the true index of cost of living: an interpretation of a special pair of equations," Comm. in Statistics, A(7) 9(1978), 851-856. [This note has later been slightly ammended, vide Comm. in Statistics, A9(1) (1980).].

[9B] Banerjee, K. S: "Wald's true index derived ipso facto," Comm. in Statistics, A7(8) (1978), 791-798.

[9C] Banerjee, K. S: "Index numbers of prices and quantities for an arbitrary number of periods," Applied Mathematics Institute, Univ. of Del., Technical Report No. 42A (1979).

[9D] Banerjee, K. S: "A note on the Divisia indices," Applied Mathematics Institute, Univ. of Del., Technical Report No. 46A (1979).

[9E] Banerjee, K. S: "An interpretation of the factorial indexes in the Light of Divisia integral indexes," Applied Mathematics Institute, Univ. of Del., Technical Report No. 51A (1979).

[9F] Banerjee, K. S: "A comparison of the constant-utility true index and the true index obtained through the factorial approach," Accepted for publication in Comm. in Statistics.

[10A] DeLury, D. B: Values and integrals of the orthogonal polynomials up to N=26, University of Ontario Press, Ontario (1950).

[13A] Geary, R. C: "A note on constant utility index of the cost of living," The Review of Economic Studies, Vol. 18 (1949-50), 55-66.

[13B] Gorman, W. M: "Separable utility and aggregation," Econometrica, 27(3) (1959), 469-481.

[13C] Geary, R. C: "A note on the comparison of exchange rates and purchasing power between countries," J. Roy. Stat. Soc., Series A, Vol. 121 (1958), 97-99.

[15A] Hulten, C. R: "Divisia index numbers," Econometrica, 41(6) (1973), 1017-1025.

[15B] Khamis, S. H: "A new system of index numbers for national and international purposes," J. Roy. Stat. Soc. Ser. A. 135(1) (1972), 96-121.

[15C] Klein, L. R. and Rubin, H: "A constant utility index of the cost of living," The Review of Economic Studies, 15 (1947-48), 84-87.

[15D] Khamis, S. H: "Properties and conditions for the existence of a new type of index number," Sankhyā (Series B), Vol. 32 (1970), 81-98.

---

[10] Some of these references are added at the suggestion of the members of the Editorial Board to whom I am highly grateful.

[19A] Prasad Rao, D. S: "Existence and uniqueness of a new class of index numbers," Sankhyā (Series B), Vol. 33 (1971), 341-354.

[23A] Stone, R: "Linear expenditure systems and demand analysis," Economic Journal, 64(1954), 511-527.

[25A] Theil, H: Theory and measurement of consumer demand, Vol. 1, North-Holland (1975).

[25B] Tintner, H. C. G: Econometrics, John Wiley, New York (1952), 60-61.

[26A] Vogt, Arthur: "Divisia indices on different paths," Theory and Applications of Economic Indices, edited by Eichhorn W., Henn R., Opitz O. and Shephard R. W., Physica-Verlag, Würzburg, Wien (1978).

Angewandte Statistik und Ökonometrie
Applied Statistics and Econometrics
Statistique Appliquée et Économétrie

Herausgegeben von Gerhard Tintner, Pierre Désiré Thionet, Heinrich Strecker, Robert Feron.

1. **Sydney Afriat/M. V. Rama Sastry/Gerhard Tintner**
   Studies in Correlation · Multivariate Analysis and Econometrics
   1975. 149 Seiten, kartoniert
2. **Hans-Werner Gottinger · Bayesian Analysis, Probability and Decision**
   1975. 116 Seiten, kartoniert
3. **Antoni Espasa · The Spectral Maximum Likelihood Estimation of Econometric Models with Stationary Errors**
   1977. 107 Seiten, kartoniert
4. **Peter K. Fleissner · Das österreichische Gesundheitswesen im ökonomischen, demographischen und politischen Kontext**
   Ein Simulationsmodell
   1977. 106 Seiten, kartoniert
6. **S. Sankar Sengupta/Gee-Kin Yeo · Embedded Invariants**
   A Contribution to Forecasting
   1977. 127 Seiten, kartoniert
7. **E. O. Heady/Th. M. Reynolds/D. O. Mitchell**
   An Econometric Simulation Model of the U. S. Farm Sector and its Policies and Food Exports
   1978. 61 Seiten, kartoniert
8. **C. W. J. Granger/Allan P. Andersen**
   An Introduction to Bilinear Time Series Models
   1978. 94 Seiten, kartoniert
9. **Pierre D. Thionet · Quelques problèmes concernant les sondages**
   1978. 138 Seiten, kartoniert
10. **Malvika Patel/Gerhard Tintner · Some Econometric Studies in Indian Agriculture**
    1978. 79 Seiten, kartoniert
11. **Gerhard Tintner/J. N. K. Rao/Heinrich Strecker**
    New Results in the Variate Difference Method
    1978. 102 Seiten, kartoniert
12. **V. A. Sposito/W. C. Smith/C. F. McCormick**
    Minimizing the Sum of Absolute Deviations
    1978. 60 Seiten, kartoniert
13. **Wolfgang Wertz · Statistical Density Estimation – A Survey**
    1978. 108 Seiten, kartoniert
14. **W. Pollan · The Cyclical Responsiveness of the Demand for Money and its Stability in an Open Economy** · The Case of Austria
    1978. 72 Seiten, kartoniert
15. **Bernhard Böhm · Geld und privater Konsum in Österreich**
    1978. 108 Seiten, kartoniert
16. **Peter Hackl · Testing the Constancy of Regression Models Over Time**
    1980. 132 Seiten, kartoniert

Vandenhoeck & Ruprecht in Göttingen und Zürich